Dining with Jesus

Dining with Jesus provides an insightful study guide to the most important mealtimes in the Bible. The book weaves together biblical insights with contemporary application and includes creative ideas for interaction. It will provide an excellent resource for small groups and individuals wanting a deeper encounter with Jesus Christ.

Dr Andrew Ollerton, bestselling author of *The Bible: A Story That Makes Sense of Life*

In a world of change and innovation, mealtimes remain not only a staple of life, but an effective resource for community and relationship building as well as being times of refreshment and joy: eating and drinking can be very pleasurable! In taking the theme of *Dining with Jesus*, Kate has looked at how those who ate and drank in the gospels had their lives changed: both by the personal encounter with Jesus, and as part of the way Jesus taught in parable story. This study guide gives an informative and clear picture of the historical events but goes much further: *Dining with Jesus* is as much for us today as it is a reminder of words and events 2000 years ago. Kate has written a practical and accessible guide that enables us to look at our own lives in the light of Jesus Christ – and with a subject matter most of us can relate to, we are challenged to see our lives are changed by his loving, joyful presence. The Gospel has to be true to itself – Good News, and this guide allows us to discover for ourselves and share with others more of how God's love is made real by Jesus Christ. I commend this Study Guide to small groups and individuals who are looking to deepen their understanding of the Christian faith, and who are willing to take the challenge of meeting with Jesus over a shared meal together.

Bishop of Dunedin (New Zealand), Steven Benford

Dining with Jesus

A Seven Course Bible Study Unpacking
the Key Meals Jesus Attended

Dining with Jesus

A Seven Course Bible Study Unpacking
the Key Meals Jesus Attended

Kate Jackson

CIRCLE
BOOKS

Winchester, UK
Washington, USA

JOHN HUNT PUBLISHING

First published by Circle Books, 2022
Circle Books is an imprint of John Hunt Publishing Ltd., No. 3 East St., Alresford,
Hampshire SO24 9EE, UK
office@jhpbooks.com
www.johnhuntpublishing.com
www.circle-books.com

For distributor details and how to order please visit the 'Ordering' section on our website.

Text copyright: Kate Jackson 2021

ISBN: 978 1 80341 040 1
978 1 80341 041 8 (ebook)
Library of Congress Control Number: 2021952727

A CIP catalogue record for this book is available from the British Library.

Design: Matthew Greenfield

UK: Printed and bound by CPI Group (UK) Ltd, Croydon, CR0 4YY
US: Printed and bound by Thomson Shore, 7300 West Joy Road, Dexter, MI 48130

We operate a distinctive and ethical publishing philosophy in
all areas of our business, from our global network of authors to
production and worldwide distribution.

Contents

Friendship is unnecessary, like philosophy, like art.... It has no survival value; rather it is one of those things which give value to survival. - C. S. Lewis

This book is dedicated to my Mum, my sister, Jim, Jonny and to everyone in my house group. Your continued support adds immeasurable value to my life.

Preface

After much thought I have come to a conclusion: My chickens have become archaeologists. Perhaps that sentence needs a little explaining...

There is a paddock which our chickens have access to and inside it there is, or rather there was, a small hillock. However, over time and through much digging, not only has the hillock shrunk, but a conglomeration of stones has been revealed underneath, along with a few pieces of pottery. Nothing very old, so far, but we live in hope of something older, like a Roman coin appearing one day.

The chickens of course are responsible for this, systematically digging away the layers of soil; three or four of them all lined up. This is a full body workout for them, beginning with a lot of claw scratching, which is then followed by much pecking within the loose soil for any insects they can find. From there the chickens begin their dust bath, rolling around and shaking the soil over themselves. Chicken archaeology is a very immersive experience.

So why am I telling you about this?

Well, it struck me one afternoon that studying the Bible shares a number of similarities, or at least it should do. Digging deeper into the Bible is a quest we are never going to complete this side of heaven. There will always be more to learn and for me this is exciting! Whether you are an actual archaeologist, a chicken or a reader of the Bible, you are going to need tools to execute your task, and this is what I hope this study guide will provide for some of the key passages in the Gospels.

The aim of this guide is to help individuals and groups to grow in their understanding of the big picture, as well as the small details of the meals Jesus attended or held. A key part of this support will be in considering these dining experiences through the lens of the stories and teachings which bookend them, and the meals will also be looked at in light of parallels found in the Old Testament. Historical and social background will be fed into the chapters, but in bite sized pieces, so you can come to this book without extensive prior knowledge. In writing this guide it was important to me to encourage others in reading the Bible and I hope those using the guide gain confidence in doing so.

Each chapter concludes with questions which equip you to examine your own lives and to see how Jesus' teachings can be further incorporated into them. Christian faith, if it is to be life-altering, cannot be an academic exercise and like a muscle it needs to be stretched and engaged in consistent activity to increase its strength.

I hope this book helps you on this journey.

I would like to thank everyone who supported me in my own journey of writing this guide and for those who took the time to read it in its draft stages. Your comments and encouragement were hugely appreciated.

Whether you are just starting out in your Christian faith, or are a seasoned pilgrim, as my chickens would say: Keep Digging!

K. J.

Introduction

Mealtimes in the First Century AD

What are your mealtimes like? Fraught affairs as you attempt to juggle several tasks, and plates, at once? Is there a roar of conversation as everyone tries to share about their day? Or are they moments ensconced in front of the television, eager to find out what is happening in your favourite soap? Is it homemade food all the way, or are you King or Queen of the microwave?

In some ways mealtimes probably haven't changed very much since Jesus' time on earth. There is still the child who likes to drop their food on the floor to feed the family pet, and the one who speaks with their mouth full, spraying crumbs liberally as they talk. Even some of the food would not be poles apart, though our intake of meat is predominately higher, as during that time meat was something you ate mostly at religious festivals. Fish was a more common source of protein and two rather than three meals a day was the norm.

Yet in some respects, dining has changed significantly, in the import and meaning it is given as an activity. For Jews in the first century AD, mealtimes were closely related to your membership of a social group, who you ate with was tied up with your identity and even your moral character. Eating together as a social group[1] was a key part of maintaining and expressing the level and purity of your faith in Jewish culture, at that time, and this affected the guests at a meal, as well as the one hosting it. Offering hospitality is a practice explicitly encouraged and even commanded in the Old Testament, with early examples shown in the conduct of Abraham (Genesis 18) and Lot (Genesis 19). Indeed, hospitality towards foreigners who have come to live in their land, became a witness to the freedom God gave the Israelites when he rescued them from the Egyptians (Leviticus 19 v 33–34).

Greeting guests was a far more intricate activity in the Classical era as well, going beyond words. Those who are familiar with John 13 v 1–7, will know how crucial a step it was to ensure your guests' feet were washed on arrival. Such meals were not simply about consuming nutrients and gaining energy to go on to fuel further activities but were also very much about table fellowship. The New Living Translation Study Bible notes that 'sharing a meal with another indicated both covenantal and social equality'[2]; a theme which is highly pertinent to Chapter 1 of this Bible study, when we look at two occasions Jesus challenges who makes it on to the guest list.

Meals also have huge symbolic value for Jews. When in the form of lavish banquets, meals become a central image used by Old Testament writers to encapsulate their hope for the future, when God's kingdom would be fully manifest on earth; a time in which evil is finally expunged from the world and God's justice is completely restored and executed. For example, Isaiah 25 looks ahead to what God will do for his people:

> In Jerusalem, the Lord of Heaven's Armies will spread a wonderful feast for all the people of the world. It will be a delicious banquet with clear, well-aged wine and choice meat.[3]

The banquet symbolises God's provision and this is an image Jesus builds upon, using the metaphor of the feast to encompass all of God's promises to transform us to enter and participate in his kingdom. In particular Jesus employs the banquet motif to show how through himself, these promises were beginning to be fulfilled. Throughout this story, we will consider the varying reactions people at the time had towards this claim. Jesus' meals were far from free of dissent and division.

'Jesus uses the banquet as a metaphor for the presence of the kingdom'[4] such as in Matthew 9 v 14–17[5] and Matthew 22 v 1–10,[6] and in the Parable of the Ten Virgins, (Matthew 25 v 1-13), we are warned to make ourselves ready for Jesus' return. In the parable Jesus is portrayed as the bridegroom and his celebrated return represents the full restoration of God's kingdom on earth. It is in many passages like this, that we see the symbolism of the banquet making its way into Christian tradition and theology, which is why it is important for us to consider what lessons the meals Jesus shared have for us and our relationship with God.

The Exodus Story

As I was researching the topic for this study, I became increasingly aware of how often the story of God rescuing his people from Egypt is a theme which makes its way into the meals Jesus had. The Exodus story is not just of great importance to Jews, but also for Christians, as it is part of our story too. God has Moses tell the Israelites:

> I am the Lord. I will free you from your oppression and will rescue you from your slavery in Egypt. I will redeem you with a powerful arm and great acts of judgement. I will claim you as my own people, and I will be your God. Then you will know that I am the Lord your God who has freed you from your oppression in Egypt. I will bring you into the land I swore to give to Abraham, Isaac and Jacob. I will give it to you as your very own possession. I am the Lord! (Exodus 6 v 6–8)

From there we have the ten plagues which came upon Egypt, from the first plague of the Nile turning to a river of blood, to the tenth in which the firstborn children of Egypt died.[7] Only then did the Pharaoh agree that the Israelites could leave, and even then, he changed his mind and had his army chase after them into the desert. It took the miracle at the Red Sea to completely secure the Israelites' freedom. They had passed through one set of trials, but the wilderness was going to present a whole new set of challenges...

As followers of Jesus, it is important for us to remember that this was more than a one-off event. Looking back, we can see that it was only the beginning of God's rescue story for humanity and that ultimately it was God's plan to set us all free from the one foe we have in common: sin, which leads to death. Yet it is on the cross that Jesus confronts his own Red Sea moment, going through death and coming out the other side; with death the vanquished enemy,[8] a process powerfully explored in the Last Supper, which this study looks at in Chapter 6.

Yet it is not just in the Passover meal that we can hear echoes of the Exodus story. In the Gospel accounts of the feeding of the 5000, (see Chapter 2), there are strong parallels to the time the Israelites were in the wilderness, fed by God with manna. Later Jesus reveals that he is the bread of life,[9] the manna which will not go mouldy the next day, the manna which can do more than fill your stomach.

In the feeding of the 4000, Jesus warns against the yeast or leaven of the Pharisees and Chapter 3 explores how Jesus uses leaven as a symbol of the old way of life. The Israelites in Exodus were expected to turn away from the life of slavery they had in Egypt and learn to be God's people and 2000 years later there is still this same expectation. If you want to follow Jesus then you need to leave your old life behind; a task which we have to respond to on a daily basis. This demand sometimes produced a negative response from certain quarters; Moses was not an instant hit with the Israelite community[10] and there was more than one grumbler in the wilderness who wanted to go back to how things were.[11] Jesus, unsurprisingly, frequently created a similar, if not stronger, adverse response, this time with the religious elite. They disapproved of the Kingdom message he was teaching, and this is a conflict which comes up in the meals Jesus had. We will be looking at one such meal in Chapter 5.

Passover and the Feast of Unleavened Bread

The rescuing of the Israelites from Egypt was so important, in what it represented and in what it now meant for the Israelites, that God instructed the Israelites to commemorate it in what is now known as the Passover meal or Passover Seder. God gave precise details[12] as to how the meal should be prepared, in particular the lamb and the bread, and also what was to be done with the lamb's blood. In Exodus 12 v 7 the Israelites are told to take some of the lamb's blood and 'smear it on the sides and top of the doorframes of the houses where they eat the animal'. This instruction was given for a very good reason which is provided in verse 13:

> [T]he blood on your doorposts will serve as a sign, marking the houses where you are staying. When I see the blood, I will pass over you. The plague will not touch you when I strike the land of Egypt.

The plague in question was the final one, the death of firstborn children, and the blood prevented the Israelite households from coming under that judgement. Beyond the practical reasons for the instruction, it is also a deeply symbolic one as the lamb's blood became a form of atonement for the Israelites' sins. Yet as Richard Booker notes, this blood 'could only cover their sins, it could not take them away'.[13] Moreover, as I said above, this was just the beginning of God's rescue plan, but to look at the direction it was heading in, we need to take a wider and deeper look at the Passover.

Passover is more than just a meal, it is a season, occurring during Nisan (March–April), and during this time three Jewish festivals take place: the Passover Meal, the week-long Feast of Unleavened Bread and the Feast of the First Fruits. 'At festivals, Israel celebrated God's work in the past, present, and future and reaffirmed its relationship with this covenantal God.'[14] In fact,

Booker points out how God 'used visual aids as object lessons to teach people specific truths'.[15] This is a helpful way to look at the Jewish feasts and festivals, as within them are important truths, which God wanted to remind the Israelites. Booker goes on to write that:

> God gave these visual aids in the Hebrew Scriptures (Old Testament part of the Bible) in the form of various religious laws and rituals which the Jews were to observe. As the Jews practised these laws and rituals, they would learn through their physical senses, spiritual truths concerning their relationship with God.[16]

The final aim of these aids was to show the way to the Messiah and his arrival on earth, which is why it is important to consider the many times Jesus identifies himself with these earlier aids and signs. Booker sums it up well when he says that Jesus was 'God's ultimate visual aid' as it is through Jesus that we can come to know the nature of God. (see John 14 v 6–11 and Colossians 1 v 15)

So, what does the Passover meal have to say about our 'relationship with God'? By saving the Israelites from death, through the sign of the lamb's blood, this also paved the way for the Israelites to be *in* relationship with God and to 'find God's peace'.[17] As we will go on to explore in Chapter 6, the Passover meal is a powerful symbolic representation of Jesus' death on the cross; a final and ultimate sacrifice which enabled our sins to be completely forgiven. This in turn allowed us to be fully reconciled with God, as well as having access to God's peace and to be at 'peace with God'.[18] Paul brings this all together in Romans 5 v 1: 'Therefore, having been justified by faith, we have peace with God through our Lord Jesus Christ...' In a nutshell the Passover meal enabled the Israelites to consider the process involved in making a relationship with God possible, and to also point ahead to the ultimate solution – Jesus.

In the Gospel accounts it is clear that Jesus is trying to make his followers and others listening to him, understand the parallels between his life and forthcoming death and the Passover meal. Not only in what he says, but also in his personal itinerary leading up to his arrest and death. It is no coincidence that 'Jesus was set aside to be sacrificed, examined and crucified on the exact month, day and hour that the Jews had been handling the lambs for 1,500 years in keeping the Feast of the Passover.'[19] Chapter 6 encourages and supports readers in exploring these parallels more closely.

I don't know about you, but when I've been reading accounts of the Last Supper, I have often wondered why it is sometimes said that the diners reclined whilst partaking of the meal. As a child, sitting up straight at the dinner table was always considered the correct thing to do. Primary school left me with the strong impression that reclining at dinner was a decidedly Roman activity, though of course it was a much more widely employed lifestyle choice in the ancient world. But how did it make its way into Jewish feasting habits? Interestingly, it was not a custom that began from the very earliest celebrations of the Passover. In Exodus 12 v 11 regarding this meal, the Israelites are told:

> These are your instructions for eating this meal: Be fully dressed, wear your sandals, and carry your walking stick in your hand. Eat the meal with urgency, for this is the Lord's Passover.

Yet by the Second Temple era, (516 BC–70 AD), a switch to reclining at the Passover meal was made; a switch which contains a further echo of the Exodus story. Rabbi Levi in the Pesachim[20] said that 'because it is the way of slaves to eat standing up' but at the Passover meal we are 'here to eat reclining, [it is] made known that they went from slavery to freedom'.[21] In passages such as this one we see how reclining when eating was used as a way of symbolising the freedom the Israelites had gained. The couches reclined upon were known as *triclinia* and three people were usually allotted to each one. The base of the couch was made of stone or wood and cushions were placed on top. The most important position belonged to the host and it was on the triclinium on the left-hand side. Jesus' warnings about the pitfalls of trying to claim the best place at the dinner spring to mind at this point and are explored in Chapter 4.

The second feast of the Passover season is the Feast of Unleavened Bread and in Deuteronomy 16 v 3–4 the Israelites are instructed that:

> For seven days the bread you eat must be made without yeast, as when you escaped from Egypt in such a hurry. Eat this bread – the bread of suffering – so that as long as you live you will remember the day you departed from Egypt. Let no yeast be found in any house throughout your land for those seven days.

Why did they need to remember their departure from Egypt? In keeping with what I said earlier about leaven and its sin connotations, this is a feast which is concerned with our changed condition, after atonement has taken place. It is a reminder for the Israelites, and then Christians, to put off their old way of living and lead a life separate from it. This point is reinforced by the command to keep yeast out of the home for seven days and prior to celebrating this feast Jewish homes will undergo a thorough cleaning. Again, this has relevance and direct implications for Christians as this cleaning is symbolic of the moral overhaul we need to give our own lives. The regular nature of the activity also intimates how this is not a one-off task and should occur throughout our walk with God. Paul puts it well when he writes:

> Since you have learned the truth that comes from him, throw off your old sinful nature and your former way of life, which is corrupted by lust and deception. Instead, let the Spirit renew your thoughts and attitudes. Put on your new nature, created to be like God – truly holy and righteous. (Ephesians 4 v 21–24)

This decision then to consecrate our lives and dedicate them to the way of life Jesus taught, is the final truth to be explored in the Passover season, in the Feast of First Fruits. Yet again, the physical acts of setting aside money, crops, and livestock, had the further purpose of pointing to the way we need to set aside our lives for God's kingdom.

Endnotes

1. This is also known as commensality.
2. Anon. (2008; 1996). Eating Together. In: *NLT Study Bible*. Illinois: Tyndale House Publishers. p. 1595. All subsequent references to this translation will be abbreviated to NLT.
3. See Isaiah 25 v 6. Unless otherwise mentioned, quoted scripture will be taken from the NLT translation.
4. Anon. (2013). Banquet. In: Longman III, Tremper *The Baker Illustrated Dictionary*. Michigan: Baker Books. pp. 167–168 (p. 167).
5. During Jesus' meal with Matthew, the tax collector, some of John Baptist's followers question Jesus as to why he and his followers do not fast.
6. This is the Parable of the Wedding Feast, which is explored in Chapter 4.
7. An account of the ten plagues can be read in Exodus 7 v 14 – Exodus 11 v 12.

8. A comparison that is explored by Tom Wright in *Mark for Everyone* (SPCK Publishing; 2001).

9. See John 6 v 35.

10. See Exodus 5 v 21 and Exodus 6 v 9.

11. See Exodus 16 v 3.

12. See Exodus 12 v 1–14 and 43–48 for further information.

13. Booker, R. (1987). *Jesus in the Feasts of Israel: Restoring the Spiritual Realities of the Feasts to the Church*. Pennsylvania: Destiny Image Publishers. p. 21.

14. Anon. (2013). Festivals. In: Longman III, Tremper *The Baker Illustrated Dictionary*. Michigan: Baker Books. pp. 584–590 (p. 584).

15. Booker, R (1987). p. 1.

16. *Ibid.*, p. 2.

17. *Ibid.*, p. 4.

18. *Ibid.*, p. 12.

19. *Ibid.*, p. 22.

20. The Pesachim is a part of the *Mishnah*. The *Mishnah* was completed c.200 AD and was the first collection made of the Jewish oral traditions, which concern all aspects of life, including festivals and eating practices.

21. Levi, R. Pesachim 68b:13. This can be found at: https://www. sefaria.org/Jerusalem_Talmud_Pesachim.68b.13, alongside the full Pesachim and other Jewish texts.

Study Guide Advice

Each section of the study will be focusing on one or two events, which have a meal at the heart of them. Yet these meals will not be explored in isolation and often readers will be encouraged to consider the events and teachings that precede and follow on from the key passage in question. The Gospel writers were not strangers to framing devices and the different stories these meals are sandwiched between hold great significance. It is important to look at the meals in light of these other passages.

It is also helpful to look at more than one Gospel account of an event, as the different accounts bring up new ideas to consider. The study guide will endeavour to help participants in doing this and highlight the key points to reflect upon. As well as bringing your attention to significant ideas, each study will offer you a variety of questions to discuss. Some will look at the big picture, whilst others will consider smaller, but still important details. There will also be questions which encourage you to think through the personal implications of the passage and what it might mean for your own life and walk with God. If you are reading this for personal use, you may wish to pause after reading the questions to consider your own answers before continuing.

If you are using this study guide in a group context, it would be advisable for the group leader to read through each chapter's materials before the group meets, as well as the Introduction and Getting Started sections. Group participants may appreciate receiving advance notification of the key passage(s) that will be discussed in the next meeting, so they can read the Bible extracts beforehand.

During the time your group meets it is not essential to answer all the questions within each chapter. Group needs differ and group leaders should be sensitive to these, allowing sufficient discussion time for the questions which have really resonated or impacted group members. Another part of group facilitation is to avoid discussion time becoming too digressive, as well as, encouraging all members to take part. Note the word encouraging! Try to avoid pressuring quieter group participants to contribute. A positive and reassuring discussion atmosphere is likely to be more effective.

Getting Started

Before beginning this Bible study series, you might wish to start with one of these icebreakers or thought sharing activities. Some activities can be used to help a group become more comfortable with one another if they haven't known each other very long, whilst others are simple ways of helping participants access their existing knowledge on the topic.

Getting to Know You

Below are various questions you can ask your group to get them to begin sharing about themselves. You can use these questions in varying ways. They can be asked as a whole group or group members could discuss them in pairs, before feeding back to the others. You could even write out the questions on a big piece of paper for group members to write their answers on, or use post-it notes. Decide what works best for you, but don't be afraid to be creative and try something different!

1. What is the most memorable dinner you have been to or hosted?
2. What dining habits annoy you the most?
3. If you could have dinner with any celebrity of your choice, who would you pick?
4. How has dining changed over time? Are these changes for the better or the worse?
5. What does dining with others mean to you?
6. If you could only eat the same meal for an entire year, what would it be?

What Sort of Diner Are You?

Below are 8 different types of diners. Take this short quiz to decide which type of diner you are most like, or if you're very brave, consider which type of diner someone else in the group is most like!

Are you the sort of diner who...
...spends the entire meal on their phone?

a) Rarely
b) Sometimes
c) Often
d) Always

...likes to go for the most unusual and adventurous item on the menu?

a) Rarely
b) Sometimes
c) Often
d) Always

...who covers their entire meal in a condiment such as mayonnaise or tomato sauce, regardless of what the food is?

a) Rarely
b) Sometimes
c) Often
d) Always

...finishes their meal first?

a) Rarely
b) Sometimes
c) Often
d) Always

…wishes they had picked what someone else is eating?

a) Rarely
b) Sometimes
c) Often
d) Always

…sneaks food off the plates of others? (Chips tend to be the most common victim of this cuisine-based crime!)

a) Rarely
b) Sometimes
c) Often
d) Always

…picks the same option on the menu each time you go to a particular restaurant?

a) Rarely
b) Sometimes
c) Often
d) Always

…takes the longest to decide what they want to order?

a) Rarely
b) Sometimes
c) Often
d) Always

So which ones were you most like? Has the type of diner you are changed over time?

Meals of the Bible: Quiz

Take this quiz to see how well you know the meals of the Bible.

1. In Genesis 18 Abraham is visited by the Lord in the form of three men. Sarah his wife is preparing food for the meal, but why does she laugh when she overhears the men talking?

2. What does Esau sell his birthright to his brother Jacob for?

3. Where does God prepare a meal, for the speaker of Psalm 23?

4. What was unusual about the bread Abimelek, the priest, offered to David and his men when they arrived exhausted at Nob? (This is written about in 1 Samuel 21.)

5. Why does Esther prepare two banquets?

6. What animals could the Israelites offer for sacrifice?

7. When Elijah goes to the Kerith Ravine in 1 Kings 17, which birds provide him with food?

8. What animals were the Israelites commanded not to eat?

9. Who did Isaac prepare a feast for in Genesis 26?

10. What does the Father in the Parable of the Lost Son command to be killed when his younger son returns home?

11. On what occasion did King Solomon sacrifice 22,000 cattle and 120,000 sheep and goats?

12. What does the neighbour ask for in the Parable of the Friend at Night? (This is told in Luke 11 v 5–8.)

13. What two foods does God provide the Israelites with in the wilderness?

14. When Elijah asks the widow at Zarephath to provide him with some bread, how does she respond? And what miracle occurs?

15. What would Daniel, Hananiah, Mishael and Azariah not eat in Daniel 1?

Answers

1. The men say she is going to have a baby and she doesn't believe it is possible, given her age.

2. He sold his birthright for a bowl of stew. (See Genesis 25 v 29–34.)

3. In the presence of the speaker's enemies. (See Psalm 23 v 6.)

4. The bread was a special kind set apart and consecrated, known as the Bread of the Presence. Ordinarily it could only be eaten by the priests. This is an incident which comes up in the teachings of Jesus in Matthew 12 v 1–8.

5. She prepares two banquets for her husband, King Xerxes, and his important official Haman in order to request the King to spare the lives of herself and the other Jews in his kingdom. Thus countering the orders given earlier by Haman to exterminate them.

6. Examples include bulls, sheep, goats and doves. Grain, meal and wine were also a part of the sacrificial offerings.

7. Ravens

8. Examples include camels, vultures, eagles, pigs, rabbits, rats and lizards. (See Leviticus 11 for further details.)

9. Abimelek and the meal was part of a ceremony to officialise an agreement made between them.

10. A fatted calf. (See Luke 15 v 11–31, for the full story.)

11. The dedication of the Temple in Jerusalem. (See 2 Chronicles 7.)

12. Three loaves of bread, as they had an unexpected guest.

13. Manna and Quail. (See Exodus 16.)

14. Initially she is reluctant to make him any bread as she only has a little flour and oil left. In fact, she had only enough to make one more meal for herself and her son. However, she does as Elijah asks and a miracle occurs with her flour and oil supplies not running out until it

began to rain again. (See 1 Kings 17.)

15. They would not eat the royal food and wine, as they felt they would be defiled by it. Perhaps because it was not kosher or had been offered to idols first. Instead, they ate vegetables and drank water.

Chapter 1

Come and Dine

Jesus Dines with Matthew and Zacchaeus

Here I am! I stand at the door and knock. If anyone hears my voice and opens the door, I will come in and eat with that person, and they with me.[1]

It is often said that we are known by the company that we keep. The people we choose as friends affects the type of influences we have in our lives. Proverbs 13 v 20 says 'walk with the wise and become wise; associate with fools and get into trouble.' Whilst 1 Corinthians 15 v 33, quoting the Greek poet Menander, warns that 'bad company corrupts good character.'

But this is only one side of the coin or one half of the picture when we consider the kind of company Jesus kept. As we will see in this chapter, Jesus' mission was to come alongside those in need of God's grace, and he clearly demonstrates that you cannot do this by holding such people at arm's length. Rather than Jesus being corrupted by the bad practices of those around him, it is shown instead that his own goodness infected them, and in such a powerful way that drastic lifestyle choices were made. Those familiar with Zacchaeus' story will remember the big promises he makes to compensate those he cheated. Yet we have to ask ourselves this question: Would Zacchaeus have so radically altered the direction of his life if Jesus hadn't invited himself to dinner?

Ice Breaker Questions

Tax collectors were not popular in the time of Jesus. What jobs today provoke a similarly strong negative reaction? Why do they prompt this response?

What lengths have you gone to, to see someone or do something, even if it meant risking looking foolish?

Key Scriptures to be Read
Matthew 9 v 9–13
Luke 19 v 1–10

Perhaps one of the most remembered details from these two stories is that Matthew and Zacchaeus were both Jewish tax collectors.

But why were such people so disliked by their fellow Jews?

The disapproval towards tax collectors has several roots. The right to collect taxes was leased by the Roman authorities to someone such as Zacchaeus, a chief tax collector. He would have put in the highest bid to gain this right. However, he would not have been out of pocket. Zacchaeus would have overseen 'subordinate tax collectors from whom he collected a commission'[2] as the NLT Study Bible points out. Moreover, 'anything collected above the bid was profit for the collectors'[3] so it is easy to see how people working in this industry quickly gathered a reputation as extortionists. Even outside the Jewish community, it was seen as exceptional for a tax collector to be honest, with one such person, Sabinus, (father to the Emperor Vespasian), being honoured with statues in several cities that were inscribed with the epitaph: 'To the honest tax collector.'[4]

Jewish tax collectors would also have been held in poor repute because 'they handled currency with blasphemous pagan inscriptions and iconography and cooperated with'[5] the Roman occupiers. William Lane suggests that the social ostracism these tax collectors experienced would have gone even further as:

When a Jew entered the customs service he was regarded as an outcast from society: he was disqualified as a judge or a witness in a court session, was excommunicated from the synagogue, and in the eyes of the community his disgrace extended to his family.[6]

What impact do you think this would have had on these men?

Take a moment to consider the potential mental and emotional consequences. What might it have been like when they encountered the first painful sting of rejection? What defences or mental walls might they have developed, over time, to numb the pain?

I am not wishing to exonerate any wrongdoing these tax collectors may have done, but I think it is important to examine the mindset of such a person before they crossed paths with Jesus, who went against the tide of common opinion and decided to get to know them.

Jesus and Matthew

Read through Matthew 9 v 9–13 before looking at the questions below.

What actions does Matthew undertake once he hears Jesus' invitation to follow him?

Verse 9 concludes with the words, 'So Matthew got up and followed him.' So simple, yet so full of meaning. Echoing the Exodus story, Matthew, in a very literal way, leaves his old way of life behind him. Nevertheless, in verse 10 we should note that this does not mean he abandons his old friends, since he invites them to dinner with Jesus, the one who radically changed his life for the better. But then why wouldn't he want the same for his friends too? Tom Wright translates the final sentence of verse 9 as, 'And he rose up and followed him'[7] and in his commentary for this episode, Wright points out how this line utilises a word commonly associated with the resurrection.[8] This emphasises the deep-rooted nature of the changes Jesus' meeting with Matthew had, and it also looks ahead to what Jesus went on to accomplish on the cross.

Why was it so important to the Pharisees who they ate with?

To understand their reasons, we need to revise our knowledge of who the Pharisees were and what they were trying to achieve. Popular culture, over time, has arguably developed an ingrained image of the Pharisees as the cartoon-like 'baddies' of the New Testament. But this is too simplistic a label. Perhaps it might even surprise you that Jesus and the Pharisees actually agreed on a number of points. Not only did the Pharisees believe in resurrection, (unlike the Sadducees), but they were also keenly waiting for the arrival of the prophesied Messiah.[9] In fact, Tom Wright and Michael Bird suggest that 'Jesus' debates with the Pharisees would be better seen as torrid insider debates between different visions of the same goal: the coming of God's kingdom on earth as in heaven.'[10]

In addition, another important similarity between Pharisaic ideas and what Jesus was trying to do, is that the Pharisees believed God's presence was 'accessible in a number of places, not just a fixed location',[11] e.g., the Temple in Jerusalem. In the Pirkei Avot,[12] a collection of Rabbinical teachings, it is written that 'if two sit together and study Torah, the Divine Presence rests between them.'[13] This idea resonates with Jesus' own message. For example, the Samaritan woman, whom he meets at the well, asks 'why is it that you Jews insist that Jerusalem is the only place of worship, while we Samaritans claim it is here at Mount Gerizim, where our ancestors worshipped?'[14] To this Jesus replies:

> Believe me, dear woman, the time is coming when it will no longer matter whether you worship the Father on this mountain or in Jerusalem. You Samaritans know very little about the one you worship, while we Jews know all about him, for salvation comes through the Jews. But the time is

coming—indeed it's here now—when true worshipers will worship the Father in spirit and in truth. The Father is looking for those who will worship him that way.[15]

The Rabbinic saying also chimes in with Paul's rhetorical question in 1 Corinthians 3 v 16: 'Don't you realise that all of you together are the temple of God and that the Spirit of God lives in you?'

So, you may ask, why were there so many altercations between the Pharisees and Jesus in the Gospels? Surely, they should be on the same side? Well one of the key reasons why the Pharisees often disputed with Jesus is because of their differing ideas on *how* God's kingdom would come to earth. Wright and Bird note that the Pharisees in the Herodian era, were 'politically marginalised' and therefore:

> became largely concerned with manufacturing the conditions necessary for Israel's eschatological restoration through a strict regime of Torah observance as seen from within their specific tradition [...] They were a Jewish renewal movement, seeking to draw Israel towards the conditions that would hasten its restoration before God and its elevation over the surrounding nations.[16]

Purity was a key element of the required conditions, in the eyes of the Pharisees, who saw the Babylonian exile, as the consequence of Israel failing 'to observe the Mosaic law at both individual and corporate levels'.[17] Moreover, Risa Kohn and Rebecca Moore suggest that because the Pharisees believed God was available outside of the Temple, that Israel 'must be ready, and in state of purity, for the encounter with God'.[18] Wright and Bird also bring up the idea that purifying rituals 'were not simply "about" personal cleanliness' but also 'symbolised the political struggle to maintain Jewish identity and to realise the dream of national liberation'.[19]

In contrast, Jesus' kingdom message 'did not reinforce, but rather called into question, the agenda of revolutionary zeal that dominated the horizon of the leading group within the Pharisees'.[20] Furthermore, Jesus' teachings about God's grace being a gift no one could earn, which we see in the Parable of the Prodigal Son, clash with the underlying Pharisaic idea that a personal and collective effort to adhere more fully to the Torah and the subsequent oral teachings, would achieve the inauguration of God's kingdom on earth. Instead, Jesus suggests this is insufficient[21] and that the Laws of Moses were a signpost towards his own arrival and God's permanent strategy for enabling his people to be made right in his eyes. In addition, Jesus frequently pulled the Pharisees up for hypocritical behaviour; appearing righteous on the outside, whilst being blind to and concealing their sinful thoughts, feelings and motivations.[22]

This need to remain in a 'state of purity' also gave the Pharisees a different definition of what it meant to be set apart for God. For them it placed very strict limitations on how they could and could not interact with non-Jews. Robert Gundry specifies further that 'a Pharisee could not eat in the house of a "sinner" (a flagrant violator of the Law) but might entertain a sinner in his own home. Yet he had to provide clothes lest the sinner's own clothes be ritually impure.'[23] Consequently, we can see why the Pharisees would have been so against Jesus dining in the homes of people such as Matthew, and why they used such vitriolic language, as 'scum' to refer to such people in verse 11 of the passage. C. J. Conner sums it up well when he writes that the Pharisees, 'couldn't get their hands dirty'[24] and this would be a real stumbling block for them, when it came to accepting, not just the way Jesus taught his message about God's kingdom, but who he taught it to.

How do Jesus' actions in this passage turn upside down the

system the Pharisees had developed?

Jesus was an observant Jew. In Matthew 5 v 17 he says, 'Don't misunderstand why I have come. I did not come to abolish the law of Moses...' Yet as the NLT Study Bible puts it, 'he regularly, purposefully, and offensively ate with those who were ritually unclean or whose commitment to law was inferior'[25] and he did it for a very good reason. Offering table fellowship to such people not only broke down social divisions but was a powerful enactment of 'God's grace – he extended God's love and forgiveness, welcoming open participation in a new society'.[26] In an act many Jews, at the time, would have thought of as defiling, deep reaching change is achieved. Yet it is only accomplished through relationship.

Jesus then goes on to further challenge the Pharisees in verse 13, by quoting Hosea 6 v 6: 'For I desired mercy, and not sacrifice; and the knowledge of God more than burnt offerings.' Given their dedication to reading God's word, this passage should have been familiar to the Pharisees. However, Jesus is questioning their understanding of this verse, even saying to them, 'go and learn the meaning of this Scripture.' It is as though he is asking them: Do you act with mercy? Do you really know God's heart? With words like 'scum' still ringing in the ears of the dinner guests, the answer seems to be no.

What does the imagery of Jesus as a doctor and sinners as sick people, say about the Pharisees' attitude towards those they considered unclean?

Wright's response to this explores the tension between keeping oneself morally pure, whilst also getting involved in the often messy work of God's kingdom:

Because, while other religious leaders of the day saw their task as being to keep themselves in quarantine, away from possible sources of moral and spiritual infection, Jesus saw himself as a doctor who'd come to heal the sick. There's no point in a doctor staying in quarantine. He'll never do his job.[27]

Jesus and Zacchaeus

Read through Luke 19 v 1–10 before looking at the questions below.

What does Zacchaeus do to see Jesus? What trait or characteristic might this show?

Whilst the idea of a wealthy and unpopular man clambering up a tree because he is too short to see what is going on, might be quite entertaining, this part of the story is also important in revealing that when God transforms someone, he redeems qualities already placed within them. Zacchaeus is a determined man. To be a successful chief tax collector you would need to be, and in the opening of this passage we also see Zacchaeus is determined to see Jesus, and he does what is needed to achieve this goal. Yet once Zacchaeus decides to turn his life around, that determination does not disappear. Instead, it is channelled and redirected into living life Jesus' way.

Look at verse 5. What words does Jesus say to Zacchaeus? And what is conveyed in those words, beyond the literal command?

At the start of this chapter, you were asked to consider how a man like Zacchaeus might have felt, given the general dislike towards him and those who held a similar job. It is important to bear those feelings in mind when we consider the impact Jesus' words would have had on him. He has gone from being derided and insulted to being called by his name. In John 10 v 3–4, Jesus talks about the good Shepherd, he himself, who 'calls his own sheep by name', who in turn, 'follow him because they know his voice'. We can see this encounter with Zacchaeus as a demonstration of this message, especially when we consider

Zacchaeus' subsequent reactions. He is not coerced into changing his life, he is offered an invitation. By stating that he 'must be a guest in' Zacchaeus' home, Jesus is not being a presumptuous dinner guest; he is extending an invitation to have a relationship with him.

Looking at verse 5 in another way, what does Jesus not say to Zacchaeus?

Zacchaeus was no saint. He had many sins and failings, which separated him from God, as well as his fellow Jews. Yet Jesus makes no mention of these. You might have expected he would. The people mentioned in verse 7 certainly would have done. They were very 'displeased' with Jesus' approach of giving the invitation first. But look at the response it elicited, as we are told in verse 6 that Zacchaeus 'took Jesus to his house in great excitement and joy' and from those feelings we find in verse 8 that Jesus' invitation has produced a dramatic desire on Zacchaeus' part to change his behaviour and to right his past wrongs. A change that is wrought from within, rather than externally imposed, creates the deepest roots within a person. This is a pattern that reoccurs in many of Jesus' other encounters with sinners and David Cross notes that:

> In the Body of Christ, a godly leader should simply *offer* direction to those for whom he's responsible. If he *demands* to be followed, the outcome will be defiled by his control. As with the followers of Jesus, when He walked the earth, people must be free to say "No," even if it's not a wise choice.[28]

Not only does this emphasise the free-will component of Jesus' approach to offering salvation, but it also reminds us to evaluate how we approach witnessing to others.

Look back to the story of the rich young ruler, which can be

found in Luke 18 v 18–23. Compare this young man's response to Jesus' invitation to Zacchaeus. How do they differ?

Zacchaeus was reviled and unscrupulous when it came to collecting taxes. The rich young ruler had kept 'the commandments since [he] was young'. Zacchaeus asks nothing of Jesus. The rich young ruler asks what he should 'do to inherit eternal life?' These two men are poles apart socially and the rich young ruler is openly asking how he needs to improve. You would expect him to be the one most open to the invitation Jesus offers. Yet he is not.

It is important to consider the reasons why Zacchaeus found it easier to give up his old lifestyle and much of his wealth. Some have suggested that it was simply because Zacchaeus had to give up less and in fact gets to decide how much compensation he offers his customers. However, as the NLT Study Bible points out:

> Normal restitution for a wrong committed was to add twenty percent to the value of the goods lost,[29] though the penalty for theft of an animal was four or five times its value.[30] Zacchaeus apparently regarded his financial gains as theft and promised the required restitution.[31]

Zacchaeus, on his own initiative, gives back more than is necessary. This leads us to consider the differing attitudes Zacchaeus and the rich young ruler may have had towards money. The rich young ruler, given his respectability and his social standing, may not have felt he needed to do much more to improve his life. Perhaps he expected a quick and easy task that he could complete and cross off his to-do list. So, we can imagine his surprise when Jesus incisively exposes his well-concealed flaw; namely his relationship towards his money. You could argue it had a much tighter grip on the rich young ruler than it did on Zacchaeus. For the rich young ruler his money may have been tightly bound with his self-image and identity, as well as representing security, status, respect, even God's approval and blessing. Jesus challenges all of this. Is it more valuable than being in a right relationship with God? Whilst the rich young ruler's reluctance to part with his money suggests it was, in Zacchaeus' actions we see the opposite response. For him acceptance from God is worth the loss of financial comfort, perhaps because he was in greater need of knowing he had acceptance than the rich young ruler who already had society's respect and approval.

What parallels are there between this story and the account of Jesus dining with Matthew?

Commenting on the story of Zacchaeus, Wright points out how it:

> fits in to three of Luke's regular themes: the problem of riches and what to do about it, the identification of Jesus with 'sinners,' and the faith which recognises Jesus as Lord and discovers new life as a result.[32]

Yet the last two themes are also ones which resonate with Jesus' encounter with Matthew. Moreover, in both stories there is a body of discontentment directed at the fellowship Jesus is offering Matthew and Zacchaeus. Jesus' personal and grace first approach to dealing with sin, which leads to him socialising with social outcasts, in each case goes against the cultural grain. You could say there is a geographical precedent as Zacchaeus' meal with Jesus takes place in Jericho. Jericho is most well known for being the city whose walls fell when the Israelites marched around them, praising God, and in Zacchaeus' story we can see walls of another kind being brought down. We also see in Joshua 6 how God uses Rahab, the prostitute, another social outcast, to aid Israelite spies and her support exonerated her from the judgement that was to befall Jericho. God's rescue plan for humanity frequently involves those on the margins of society.

Jesus' meals with Matthew and Zacchaeus also place Jesus in the driving seat when it comes to an individual's salvation. In both stories Jesus makes a point to find these men and in Luke 19 v 10, he says he 'came to seek and save those who are lost'. So not only is it Jesus who does the searching, (reminding us of the three parables of the lost things,[33]) but it is also he who does the saving, which again reinforces the gift-like nature of God's grace.

At what point does 'salvation' come to Zacchaeus?

Jesus' proclamation that 'salvation has come to this home today' is delivered once Zacchaeus has accepted Jesus and internal changes have begun to take place. Yet Zacchaeus only went on to do this because he was accepted just as he was first, his sense of self-worth restored, and that acceptance enabled him to move forward and not stay the way he was. The reference to Zacchaeus being a 'true son of Abraham', in the same verse, highlights how Zacchaeus' salvation is rooted in his belief in Jesus. In doing so this line echoes Genesis 15 v 6 which says, 'And Abram believed the Lord, and the Lord counted him as righteous because of his faith.'

Jesus and You

The questions below are there to help you consider your own walk with God and the themes raised in this chapter. These questions touch upon sensitive subjects, so remember to listen to each other's responses with consideration and care.

How has this chapter's passage challenged the way you interact with people? Reflect on your skills in accepting people where they are at. Do mercy and love come first, or does the need to 'fix' the other person take over?

This chapter also raises questions about our relationship with God and the grace he offers. Do you feel this is an area you struggle in? Is there a feeling that you need to try harder, or that you cannot be accepted if people knew you, warts and all?

How well do you extend God's grace, (through meals or other ways), to those in your social circle and wider community? How could you develop this area of your life?

You could consider supporting an organisation operating in your area, such as Crisis or the Salvation Army, whose various services aim to offer acceptance, friendship and practical assistance, to those who are marginalised and disadvantaged.

Consider your attitude towards money. How closely bound up is money with your identity and sense of self-worth? Is your sense of security strongly affected by your bank balance? You can also reflect on your approach to spending money. Are you someone who is unable to enjoy using your money for yourself? Or perhaps you struggle with the opposite difficulty of spending too much? Where do you find God fits within all of this?

Endnotes

1. Revelation 3 v 20.
2. Anon. (2008; 1996). 19:2 Footnote. In: *NLT Study Bible*. Illinois: Tyndale House Publishers. p. 1746.
3. Anon. (2008; 1996). 9:10 Footnote. In: *NLT Study Bible*. Illinois: Tyndale House Publishers. p. 1594.
4. Suetonius. (1996). Life of Vespasian 1–2. In: ed. Lomas, K. *Roman Italy, 338 BC – AD 200: A Sourcebook*. London: Routledge. pp. 124–125 (p.124).
5. Anon. (2012; 1970). *A Survey of the New Testament*. 5th ed. Michigan: Zondervan. p. 53.
6. Lane, W. (1974). *The Gospel of Mark*. Michigan: Wm. B. Eerdmans Publishing Co. pp. 101-102.
7. Wright, T. (2002). *Matthew for Everyone: Part 1*. London: SPCK. p. 99.
8. *Ibid.*, p. 102.
9. When Paul gives his defence to Agrippa in Acts 26 verses

6–8, this is the common ground he tries to develop with his Jewish listeners: 'Now I am on trial because of my hope in the fulfilment of God's promise made to our ancestors. In fact, that is why the twelve tribes of Israel zealously worship God night and day, and they share the same hope I have. Yet, Your Majesty, they accuse me of having this hope!'

10. Wright, N. T. and Michael F. Bird (2019). *The New Testament in Its World: An Introduction to the History, Literature, and Theology of the First Christians.* London: Harper Collins. p. 209.

11. Kohn, R. & Rebecca Moore (2007). *A Portable God: The Origin of Judaism and Christianity.* Plymouth: Rowman and Littlefield Publishers, Inc. p. 89.

12. Pirkei Avot is translated as Chapters of the Fathers in English. These saying are derived from many different teachers from between 200 BC and 200 AD and are interested in ethics and moral issues.

13. This quote can be found in: Wright, N. T. and Michael F. Bird (2019). *The New Testament in Its World: An Introduction to the History, Literature, and Theology of the First Christians.* London: Harper Collins. p. 209.

14. See John 4 v 19–20.

15. See John 4 v 21–23.

16. Wright, N. T. and Michael F. Bird (2019). *The New Testament in Its World: An Introduction to the History, Literature, and Theology of the First Christians.* London: Harper Collins. p. 125.

17. Anon. (2010). IX The Rise of Judaism. In: Tenney, M. C. *The Zondervan Encyclopedia of the Bible Volume 3 H–L Revised.* Michigan: Zondervan.

18. Kohn, R. & Rebecca Moore (2007). *A Portable God: The Origin of Judaism and Christianity.* Plymouth: Rowman and Littlefield Publishers, Inc. p. 89.

19. Wright, N. T. and Michael F. Bird (2019). *The New Testament*

in Its World: An Introduction to the History, Literature, and Theology of the First Christians. London: Harper Collins. p. 126.

20. Wright, N. T. and Michael F. Bird (2019). *The New Testament in Its World: An Introduction to the History, Literature, and Theology of the First Christians.* London: Harper Collins. p. 126.

21. This comes across in Jesus' encounter with the rich young ruler, (see Luke 18) and in verses such as John 14 verse 6: 'Jesus told him, "I am the way, the truth, and the life. No one can come to the Father except through me."'

22. See Matthew 23 v 13 and 23–26 for examples of this.

23. Gundry, Robert H. (2012; 1970). *A Survey of the New Testament.* 5th ed. Michigan: Zondervan. p. 86.

24. Conner, C. J. (2007). *Jesus and the Culture Wars: Reclaiming the Lord's Prayer.* Oklahoma: Tate Publishing. p. 100.

25. Anon. (2008; 1996). Eating Together. In: *NLT Study Bible.* Illinois: Tyndale House Publishers. p. 1595.

26. *Ibid.,* p. 1595.

27. Wright, T. (2002). *Matthew for Everyone: Part 1.* London: SPCK. p. 101.

28. Cross, David (2008). *Trapped by Control: How to Find Freedom.* Lancaster: Ellel Ministries. p. 23.

29. See Leviticus 5 v 16 and Numbers 5 v 7.

30. See Exodus 22 v 1.

31. Anon. (2008;1996). 19:8 Footnote. In: *NLT Study Bible.* Illinois: Tyndale House Publishers. p. 1746.

32. Wright, T. (2001). *Luke for Everyone.* London: SPCK. p. 222.

33. See Luke 15 v 1–24.

Chapter 2

Satisfying Our Hunger

Jesus Feeds the 5000

Yes, the Sovereign Lord is coming in power. He will rule with a powerful arm. See, he brings his reward with him as he comes. He will feed his flock like a shepherd.[1]

This chapter's story is one of Jesus' best-known miracles. It is a firm Sunday school favourite, and the UK Bible Society even delivered an audience interactive re-telling of the tale on Brighton beach in 2013. Jesus on this occasion is invariably regarded as kind, generous and – that deadliest of adjectives – nice. Yet as this study will help you to unpack, Jesus' mealtime miracle is about so much more. It speaks a powerful message of who Jesus is and what the Kingdom of God will be like. Reflecting upon this story and the passages which follow, an unequivocal challenge is also issued by Jesus himself, to those who follow him. In our modern age a story like this can be quickly dismissed as a childish fairy tale or be seen as something intended for biblical times, but not for now. It is all too easy to put God in a box or to miss the fact that God is still 'operating with unimpaired energy in the present and leading forward into a hopeful future'.[2] Both of these distorted viewpoints are confronted in the feeding of the 5000 and the teachings that succeed it. They depict a Messiah who is untameable and untrainable, who in turn requires the listener to re-assess their own ideas of what is doable, as well as remember that 'through God everything is possible'.[3]

Ice Breaker Questions

Describe someone in your life who you can rely on. How have

they demonstrated this quality?

What is the biggest meal you have ever had to make?

Key Scriptures to be Read

Mark 6 v 6–44

John 6 v 1–59

The passages you are recommended to read in this chapter are longer than usual, as they incorporate the events which come before and after the feeding of the 5000. It is important to not skip these events as they provide significant insights into Jesus' miracle and what he was trying to communicate through it. Remember you do not have to cover all the questions within your group session. You may wish to focus on the Gospel account your group is less familiar with, or perhaps spend two sessions looking at the story. Choose the approach that best suits your group.

Picture this: You are exhausted physically, mentally and emotionally. Lately your days have been spent meeting the needs of others. You feel drained. Your cousin has recently been beheaded. All you want is some time alone. But instead, as you step out from your boat you find a huge crowd of people eager for your help.

How do you feel in that moment? How do you respond? Would it be the same way that Jesus did?

Compassion is a key component of Jesus' response, which he felt so powerfully he was prepared to sacrifice his own comfort and needs. This is a response that we also find in many of Jesus' actions, not least in the Easter story. Interestingly the feeding of the 5000 and Jesus' resurrection are the only two miracles which all four Gospels include.

Why do you think the Gospel writers thought this event was so important?

Mirroring Jesus' death and resurrection, the Gospel of John informs us that the feeding of the 5000 took place during the Passover season.[4] The Passover celebrations were born out of the Israelites' rescue from the Egyptians, as told in the book of Exodus. Their rescue also entailed a long excursion in the wilderness. God used this time to demonstrate his ability to provide for his people, as well as give them the opportunity to grow into their new identity as God's people and the responsibilities this calling held. One example of God's care for the Israelites during this time can be seen in his regular provision of quail and bread (often known as manna).[5] The parallels between the Israelites' time in the desert and Jesus' feeding of the 5000 are not accidental and John's Gospel in particular encourages readers to see Jesus' miracle in light of the earlier Exodus story. The God who 'once delivered his people through the waters and provided manna for them in wilderness [...] is once again delivering and providing for his people through Jesus'.[6]

Getting Involved
Re-read Mark 6 v 35–37 and John 6 v 5–7

Before we get into Jesus' role and identity more deeply, it is important to consider how the disciples are involved in this story. Whilst the feeding of the 5000 is Jesus' miracle, he chooses to include the disciples in the process, foreshadowing the way in which Jesus intends his followers to be ambassadors for God's kingdom. Jesus reinforces this point in John 15 v 1–8, when he describes the relationship between God and his people as the vine and the branches. In particular he says, 'Yes, I am the vine; you are the branches. Those who remain in me, and I in them, will produce much fruit. For apart from me you can do nothing.'[7] Here we can see that we are not expected to do things for God in our own strength, as coming back to the feeding of the 5000, Jesus did not expect the disciples to already possess or go out and obtain enough money to feed all of the people. But Jesus did want to work with what they already had: the five loaves, the two fish and their faith in him. This principle still operates in the lives of believers today.[8]

How do the disciples respond to Jesus' invitation to get involved in solving this catering crisis?

Astonishment is one word to describe their reaction, as they exclaim the impracticalities of finding all the money needed to buy such a large amount of food. Yet Jesus' command is clear – 'You feed them.'[9] This is not the first time God has challenged his followers' perceptions of what is possible. In 2 Kings 4 v 42–44 we find another mealtime dilemma, of too many people and too little food. During a time of famine, a man comes to Elisha with 20 loaves of bread and Elisha commands him to feed the 100 people who are with them. Like Jesus' disciples the man is confounded by the instruction, as he no doubt mentally divided the 20 loaves between the 100 people. Nevertheless, Elisha is insistent and in verse 43 declares that 'the Lord says: Everyone will eat and there will even be some left over!' Unsurprisingly God fulfils his promise with abundance, and this event anticipates Jesus' much larger demonstration of such a miracle. Again, it was not the job of the man to make the food go further, his task was to be obedient to the instruction he was given.[10] It was down to God to feed the people. So, we can see in both feeding miracles that these are faith stretching opportunities, which encourage believers to increase their reliance on God to do what they cannot possibly do by themselves. Importantly, each occasion also shows that the more we rely on God, the scale of what we can achieve increases in size exponentially.

Gospel of Mark

Read Mark 6 v 6–13

What have the disciples been tasked with doing?

Tucked away at the beginning of chapter 6, it can be easy to forget that prior to the feeding of the 5000, the disciples had been able to 'cast out many demons' and had 'healed many sick people' using Jesus' authority.

In light of these earlier events, are you surprised by the disciples' narrow thinking when faced with the 5000 hungry people? Why do the disciples seem to rely more on their own abilities in this instance?

Perhaps this moment shows us how easy it is to forget the amazing things God has already done for or through us, and how important it is that we take steps to remember these things.

Re-read Mark 6 v 14–29

Compare Herod's banquet with Jesus' feast with the 5000. Why do you think Mark placed these events back-to-back? What connections are we supposed to make?

One meal might have been more luxurious and indulgent than the other, but only one feast had a real king as host. Despite locally being called a king, Herod Antipater, (nicknamed Antipas), was only ever a tetrarch or governor of Galilee and Perea, which meant he could only hold his leadership role as long as the Romans allowed him to.[11] Preventing riots and revolutions was therefore a big priority for Herod and his insecurity over his position arguably contributed to his efforts to appease the conflicting political and religious groups around him. It is not hard to see the differences between Herod and Jesus, with self-interest on the one side, and self-sacrifice on the other.

Herod's party also reveals other aspects of his character. He is a man easily swayed by the wishes of others, to the point of committing injustices, and he is someone who can be made to feel uncomfortable about his immoral behaviour, but not enough that he wants to repent of such actions and change. Herod was desperate to be seen as a king, and not lose face, whilst Jesus backed away from the designs of others to make him a king in the earthly sense.[12] It is telling that in Mark 6 v 34 Jesus sees the people as 'sheep without a Shepherd'. This indictment of Herod's leadership and of the religious authorities has strong roots in the Old Testament, which frequently depicts Israel in this manner.[13] Ezekiel 34 deploys this image extensively, itemising in verses 1–8 the ways in which Israel's spiritual and political leaders were failing the people of Israel on the one hand, whilst enumerating on the other, in verses 11–24, God's promises for his people, as the good shepherd. Jesus' actions throughout his time on earth show themselves to be a working out of these promises and the connection between Jesus' words in Mark 6 and Ezekiel 34 is reinforced in the way Jesus reiterates the declaration of Ezekiel 34 v 5 that 'my sheep have been scattered without a shepherd.' Furthermore, in this Old Testament passage, God specifically promises that he will feed his sheep 'on the mountains', 'give them good pastureland on the high hills' and feed them 'in the lush pastures of the hills'.[14] Not only does the geographical references to hills and mountains resonate with the area in which Jesus feeds the 5000, but in Mark 6 v 42 it says that the people 'ate as much as they wanted'. Their needs were met in full.

Re-read Mark 6 v 41–44

Which words foreshadow the Last Supper?

The feeding of the 5000 not only alludes to Israel's past, but it also looks forward into the future to the Last Supper, in which Jesus also breaks the bread before distributing it, and further still to the messianic banquet in which God's kingdom is completely unfolded upon earth, as mentioned in Revelation. In both the

Last Supper and this meal with the 5000, the bread handed out has a greater meaning than its practical value, which can be seen in the amount of bread left over afterwards. The twelve baskets of bread at their simplest demonstrate the rich generosity of God and bring to mind Jesus' words in John 10 v 10, which *The Passion Bible* translates as: 'But I have come to give you everything in abundance, more than you expect – life in its fullness until you overflow!' This promise is evident in the feeding of the 5000 and Jesus' discussion of the miracle afterwards, (which we will explore in the next section). After all, the disciples end up with more food than they started with, a beautiful example of the way the kingdom of God turns things upside down.

Commentators such as Tom Wright have also put forward the idea that 'the twelve baskets [of bread] left over may point to Jesus' intention to restore God's people, the twelve tribes of Israel.'[15] Throughout the Bible the number twelve is used to symbolise the complete body of God's people and Jesus' selection of twelve disciples reinforces this meaning. Moreover, when it comes to twelve baskets of leftover bread, we can look back to Leviticus 24 v 5–9, in which the Israelites are given instructions on the making and use of the Showbread/Bread of the Presence. Twelve loaves were instructed to be made and in verse 8 it is said that 'the bread is to be received from the people of Israel as a requirement of the eternal covenant.' As mentioned in the introduction to this Bible study, God often used rituals in the Old Testament as a way of communicating specific truths to the Israelites and to also point ahead to the arrival of Jesus, the 'bread of life'.[16] The Showbread was symbolic of God's presence amongst his people and his commitment to provide for them and maintain a covenantal relationship.[17] This would take on additional meaning after the Babylonian Exile when there would be a growing hope 'that the twelve tribes would be restored'.[18] Yet, as stated at the beginning of this chapter, Jesus was trying to show those around him that God was beginning to implement his plan to restore his people and that he was doing so through Jesus himself.

Gospel of John

John regards the feeding of the 5000 as a sign, but what do you think Jesus was trying to tell us through it?

John's account of this event helps us to explore more deeply how Jesus' miracles functioned as signs. Matthew C. Williams writes that:

> signs *signify* something more glorious than the miracles themselves [...] Signs show us that the loving God is active and interested in his creation. When a sign is seen correctly, it leads to faith in Jesus as God's agent of salvation. They do not, however, coerce faith.[19]

This last point is of particular importance. Jesus, contrary to the Roman emperors of the time, who employed bread and circuses[20] to maintain citizen loyalty, is not interested in gaining followers through bribery. God's generosity is abundant, but as we are to see this does not mean he can be treated like a vending machine. In John 6 v 26 Jesus challenges this attitude head-on saying, 'I tell you the truth, you want to be with me because I fed you, not because you understood the miraculous signs.' Wright sums it up well when he asserts that 'what matters is not just what Jesus can do for you; what matters is who Jesus is.'[21]

Moreover, Wright, who interprets the feeding of the 5000 as 'a sign of new creation'[22] goes on to explain that:

> What we call Jesus' 'miracles' were not done as acts of supernatural power, in order to show that there was a God who had such power, who was operating through Jesus and who could (if he chose) solve all problems with a snap of the conjurer's fingers. The mighty acts of Jesus were not that

sort of thing at all. They were about the breaking in of God's kingdom in and through Jesus, a complex event which would reach its full climax in his death and resurrection. From that point there would go out into all the world the power of new creation; but it would always have to struggle against the still-resistant forces of evil.[23]

Jesus's life and death initiated the kingdom of God on earth and the promises of a new creation as mentioned in Revelation 21 v 1. As told in 2 Corinthians 5 v 17, 'anyone who belongs to Christ has become a new person. The old life is gone; a new life has begun.' Yet God's work in us and the completion of his kingdom upon earth will not be wholly fulfilled until Christ's return. Vern Poythress notes that:

> we can see the same pattern of inaugurated and consummated new creation with the miracle of feeding the 5000. The miracle depicts the way in which Jesus is the bread of life to those who believe in him. But the food that we have from him now is also an anticipation of the consummation of being fed fully: we look forward to the marriage supper of the Lamb. (Rev. 19:9)[24]

Jesus reinforces this point in John 6 v 35 when he says 'whoever comes to me will never be hungry again. Whoever believes in me will never be thirsty'; a promise which looks ahead to the full establishment of God's kingdom on earth.

In John 6 v 14, the people proclaim that Jesus 'is the prophet we have been expecting' which alludes to Deuteronomy 18 v 15 in which Moses tells the Israelites that 'the Lord your God will raise up for you a prophet like me from among you, from your fellow Israelites.' The New Testament sees Jesus as that long-awaited prophet.

What similarities can you see between Jesus and Moses?

The actions of Jesus and Moses reveal several parallels, one of which is heralded by the closing remarks of Deuteronomy 34: 'There has never been another prophet in Israel, like Moses, whom the Lord knew face to face.'[25] Both of these prophets had an intimate relationship with God, a relationship which allowed them to mediate on the behalf of others with God and to intercede for them. Moses held a crucial role in the redeeming of God's people from slavery in Egypt. Yet as we switch our attention to Jesus, we can see that Moses' life was a signpost to the greater things Jesus was going to do. Jesus too was going to save God's people from slavery, but this time it was from being enslaved to sin and death.[26] Through accepting Jesus' death on the cross we have access to God the father and we are able to escape God's judgement, as we are told that 'Christ Jesus died for us and was raised to life for us, and he is sitting in the place of honour at God's right hand, pleading for us' (Romans 8 v 34).

You can see how in the feeding of the 5000, Jesus' actions were awakening the awareness of those around him to the Old Testament promises of Exodus. Nevertheless, as we will see he was also trying to show them that better things were coming…

Re-read John 6 v 22–59

What do the crowd want Jesus to do?

Given that this was the Passover season, the Jewish people would have been re-reading the Exodus story, so the miracles Moses performed would have been fresh in their minds. The 'Jews believed that when the Messiah appeared, he would duplicate the great miracle of Moses. Manna would once again fall, and everyone would consider it a second exodus.'[27]

Why is the crowd's request to replicate the miracle of the manna in the wilderness wrongly motivated?

We have considered the parallels between Jesus and Moses,

yet a key point of this passage from John's Gospel is that Jesus does not intend to be an exact replica of Moses. The reverence for Moses in this passage is so palpable that in verse 32 Jesus has to correct their assertion that it was Moses who did the miracle. Moses performed the miracle, but the aim of that miracle was to point back to God, the one who achieved it.

In this passage Jesus is trying to shift the attention of the crowd from the literal physical and temporary benefit of the food to the much greater and longer lasting benefit that is now on offer: 'And now [God] offers you the true bread from heaven.'[28] The crowd were so focused on the signs in and of themselves that they were at risk of missing what the signs were alluding to. This encouragement to move away from the actual bread is begun earlier in verse 27 when Jesus says: 'But don't be so concerned about perishable things like food. Spend your energy seeking the eternal life that the Son of Man can give.'

During this dialogue with the crowd, in verse 35, Jesus also gives his first 'I am' saying: 'I am the bread of life.' What do you think Jesus means when he says this?

Bread was a staple part of the Jewish diet. It was an everyday and imperative food item needed to live. So in his first 'I am' saying, Jesus is positioning himself as a life essential and June Fryman writes that:

> [W]e are not satisfied spiritually unless we know Jesus; we are not spiritually satisfied unless we have Jesus in our lives. Or to be more blunt, we cannot survive spiritually without Jesus. On our own, we will try to fill ourselves with that which does not or cannot satisfy our deepest longings.[29]

It is also important to remember Jesus' own wilderness experience when he was tempted in the desert by the Devil.[30] Jesus responds to one of these temptations by quoting Deuteronomy 8 v 3:

'people do not live by bread alone; rather we live by every word that comes from the mouth of the Lord.' Yet in John 1 v 14 we are told that 'the Word became human and made his home among us.' The Word is Jesus, God incarnate, so Jesus' saying, 'I am the bread of life' binds together these ideas of him being the ultimate source of spiritual nourishment.

Yet Jesus' message is not readily accepted at this point. What expectations do the crowd have of Jesus and the long-awaited Messiah? How does Jesus frustrate these expectations?

A key idea to consider is the disparity between what the Jews felt they wanted and what the Jews actually needed. Jesus was trying to show them what they needed to be made right with God and have their spiritual hunger truly satisfied rather than temporarily satiated. In fact, their own conception of a political and military Messiah who would vanquish the Romans was short-changing themselves against what Jesus was offering them. This contrast is emphasised further when in verses 49–50 Jesus tells them, 'Your ancestors ate manna in the wilderness, but they all died. Anyone who eats the bread from heaven, however, will never die.' Throughout this passage Jesus' words on this subject frequently echo, in their earnestness, Isaiah 55 v 1–2:

> Is anyone thirsty? Come and drink – even if you have no money! Come, take your choice of wine or milk – it's all free! Why spend your money on food that does not give you any strength? Why pay for food that does you no good? Listen to me, and you will eat what is good. You will enjoy the finest food.

In this passage the crowd says to Jesus in verse 28, 'We want to perform God's works, too. What should we do?' What does Jesus say God wants them to do? Why is this so important?

The answer lies in verse 29: 'This is the only work God wants from you. Believe in the one he has sent.' This may seem like a simple request but for those listening in the crowd it would be a sentence loaded with implications. Yes, that belief would enable them to access God and to have eternal life, but they would also have to recognise 'that in Jesus, and in everything he is doing, the same God is at work who was at work in the Exodus story'.[31] This recognition, in turn, would require a significant adjustment spiritually and mentally. Old perceptions of what they thought God was going to do would have to be replaced by what Jesus was doing right there in front of them. Wright comments that:

> the crowd realise that Jesus is pointing out that they can't just expect bread on demand, that if this really is a heaven-sent renewal movement there will be a new standard to which they must sign up.[32]

Accepting Jesus as 'the bread of life' was going to entail a lot of personal change so the crowd's resistance to the idea is not surprising.

Like Mark's account of the feeding of the 5000, John also anticipates the Last Supper. A key example is when Jesus proclaims in verse 51 'I am the living bread that came down from heaven. Anyone who eats this bread will live forever; and this bread, which I will offer so the world may live is my flesh.'

How do the crowd respond to this proclamation and what do you think Jesus meant by it?

The crowd's response is an understandable one of confusion and revulsion, given the literal interpretation they give this statement. Jesus was not advocating cannibalism, nor was he trying to flout the Jewish law which tabooed the drinking of blood.[33] Jesus allowed his body to be broken and his blood to be shed on the cross and in order to have our sins forgiven this is a sacrifice we must accept and make a part of our lives. Jesus intends and even longs for us to 'profit from [his] death'[34] and when we do so that is how we drink his blood and eat his flesh. Flesh and blood represented the whole person in Jewish culture and in verse 56 of this passage Jesus says that those who partake of his flesh and blood 'remains in me and I in him'. This begins to reveal the ongoing nature and effects of eating Jesus' flesh and drinking Jesus' blood. It is not a one-off event, which Paul demonstrates when he writes that, 'my old self has been crucified with Christ. It is no longer I who live, but Christ lives in me.'[35] Just as Jesus' flesh and blood was killed and resurrected, so too are our own lives, when we commit ourselves to Jesus. Our old sinful self dies and our new self in Christ is born, though as Paula Gooder notes, this does not happen overnight and 'involves resolve, setting our minds to it and working at it day by day'.[36]

Jesus and You

The questions below are there to help you consider your own walk with God and the themes raised in this chapter. These questions touch upon sensitive subjects, so remember to listen to each other's responses with consideration and care.

Reliance, problem-solving and trust are all themes woven into this chapter, but how quickly do you turn to God when faced with a problem? Does it depend on what the problem is? Should it depend on the nature of the problem?

In *Your God Is Too Small*, J. B. Phillips writes that 'the trouble with many people today is that they have not found a God big enough for modern needs.'[37] Is this a problem you have or have had in the past? Are there or have there been problems or situations which you haven't trusted God enough to handle?

Following the feeding of the 5000, Jesus' disciples are in a boat and they see him walking on the water. Peter is invited to step out of the boat and walk on the water with Jesus. Yet none of the other disciples joined him. What stops us from getting out of the boat in our own lives?

When Elisha meets the widow in 1 Kings 4 v 1–7, she says she had 'nothing at all, except a flask of olive oil'.[38] But that was all God needed to bless her household. What resources do you have, however small, that God can use? Has your perception of their smallness discouraged you from letting God use them?

Endnotes

1. Isaiah 40 v 10–11.
2. Phillips, J. B. (1952; 2004). *Your God Is Too Small*. New York: Touchstone. p. 7.
3. See Matthew 19 v 26.
4. See the Introduction for more information. Tom Wright in *Mark for Everyone* (2001) points out how the lushness of the grass, as mentioned in Mark's account of this event, indicates a springtime setting for the feeding of the 5000.
5. See Exodus 16 v 12.
6. Anon. (2011). Sign #4 – Jesus Feeds the Five Thousand (6:1-15). In: Hays, J. and Duvall, J. *The Baker Illustrated Bible Handbook*. Michigan: Baker Books. p. 665.
7. See John 15 v 5.
8. See Philippians 2 v 13: 'For God is working in you, giving you the desire and the power to do what pleases him.'
9. See Mark 6 v 37.
10. Another example which illustrates the importance of obedience can be found in 1 Kings 17 v 7–16, in which a widow is commanded by Elijah to use the last of her resources to make him some bread. In verse 14 she is promised that her flour and oil will not run out until it begins to rain again. This promise is fulfilled, yet this blessing could only occur once the widow had been obedient to the original command.
11. *Jeffers, James S. (2000). The Greco-Roman World of the New Testament Era: Exploring the Background of Early Christianity. Illinois: Intervarsity Press. p. 125.*

12. See John 6 v 15.

13. See Numbers 27 v 17, 1 Kings 22 v 17 and Zechariah 10 v 2.

14. The quotes in this sentence come from Ezekiel 34 v 13 and 14.

15. Wright, T. (2002). *Matthew for Everyone: Part 1*. London: SPCK. p. 187.

16. See John 6 v 35.

17. Fairchild, Mary. (2019). *Table of Showbread*. Available: https://www.learnreligions.com/table-of-showbread-700114.Last accessed 15th April 2020.

18. Aus, Roger David (2010). *Feeding the Five Thousand: Studies in the Judaic Background of Mark 6:30–44 par. and John 6:1–15*. Maryland: University Press of America. p. 110.

19. William, Matthew C. (2011). Gospel of John. In: Hays, J. and Duvall, J. *The Baker Illustrated Bible Handbook*. Michigan: Baker Books. p. 664.

20. A phrase attributed to the Roman poet Juvenal, which can be found in his 'Satire X'.

21. Wright, T. (2001). *Mark for Everyone*. London: SPCK. p. 80.

22. Contrast this with Herod's banquet which ends in death.

23. Wright, T (2001). *Mark for Everyone*. London: SPCK. p. 80.

24. Poythress, Vern S. (2016). *The Miracles of Jesus: How the Saviour's Mighty Acts Serve as Signs of Redemption*. Illinois: Crossway. p. 41.

25. See Deuteronomy 34 v 10.

26. This role is flagged up early on in John's Gospel in chapter 3 v 16–17: 'For God loved the world so much that he gave his one and only Son, so that everyone who believes in him will not perish but have eternal life. God sent his Son into the world not to judge the world, but to save the world through him.'

27. Anon. (2008; 1996). 6:30 Footnote. In: *NLT Study Bible*. Illinois: Tyndale House Publishers. p. 1781.

28. See John 6 v 32.

29. Fryman, June (2018). *Meaning of 'I am the bread of life'*. Available: https://www.wnewsj.com/opinion/columns/83226/meaning-of-i-am-the-bread-of-life. Last accessed 16th April 2020.

30. See Matthew 4 v 1–11.

31. Wright, T. (2001). *John for Everyone: Part 1 Chapters 1–10.* London: SPCK. p. 80.

32. *Ibid,* p. 80.

33. See Leviticus 17 v 10–14. This rule has its origins in Genesis 9 v 4 in which God says to Noah and his family that 'you must not eat meat that has its lifeblood still in.'

34. Wright, T. (2001). *John for Everyone: Part 1 Chapters 1–10.* London: SPCK. p. 86.

35. See Galatians 2 v 20.

36. Gooder, Paula (2009). *This Risen Existence: The Spirit of Easter.* Norwich: Canterbury Press. p. 86.

37. Phillips, J. B. (1952; 2004). *Your God Is Too Small.* New York: Touchstone. p. 7.

38. See 2 Kings 4 v 2.

Chapter 3

Growing in Faith

Jesus Feeds the 4000

Yes, I am the gate. Those who come in through me will be saved. They will come and go freely and will find good pastures.[1]

Perhaps when you saw the focus of this chapter you felt a sense of déjà vu. You may have even wondered what is 'new' about this second feeding miracle. After all, didn't we cover everything in the previous chapter? Surely this is just the same miracle?

Naturally this issue has been debated a great deal, with some believing the feeding of the 5000 and the feeding of the 4000 to be the same event told twice, whilst others regard them as two separate events. This latter view gains credence within the Gospels themselves, as in both Matthew 16 v 9–10 and Mark 8 v 19–21, Jesus refers to these meals individually. Irrespective of which viewpoint you take, it is important to go into this chapter with a mind open to receiving something fresh. After each feeding miracle Jesus is keen to stress that more is at work than a temporary satisfying of physical hunger. These meals invariably become a platform for Jesus' teaching, providing him with an opportunity to invite listeners to re-examine their previously held ideas and expectations about God and his kingdom. In discussing Mark's Gospel, Larry Hurtado writes that Mark:

saw both feeding miracles as important revelations of Jesus' significance. His devoting space for two accounts of the same sort of miracle suggests that each one had for him a special significance and that neither could be omitted without losing something important.[2]

So as we explore this miracle together, let's be receptive to discovering more about Jesus and the life he wishes to offer us.

Ice Breaker Questions

1. Share one skill, piece of knowledge or 'life lesson' which took you many attempts to grasp.
2. Name one thing you found hard to let go of, or one thing you don't feel you could ever part with.

Key Scriptures to be Read

Mark 8 v 1–12
Matthew 15 v 32–37
Matthew 16 v 1–12

There has been much discussion over the theological significance of the feeding of the 4000 and the number of leftover baskets of food. Many commentators, though not all, have seen the feeding of the 5000 as a miracle for the Jews, with the twelve baskets referring to the restoration of Israel, and the feeding of the 4000 as a miracle for the Gentile community. The number seven in the Bible is frequently used to symbolise completeness, so the seven baskets of leftover food, after the feeding of the 4000, have been interpreted as a sign of God extending his covenantal relationship to include Gentiles, as well as a restored Israel. The location of this second miracle has further fed into this idea as the meal is believed to have occurred near Tyre and the fringes of the Decapolis.[3] Jesus had healed a man possessed by an evil spirit when he had last been in the area, and had commissioned the man to tell his family what God had done for him.[4] This was a locale well-populated with Gentiles, though not exclusively, and as we will unpack later, the story of the feeding of the 4000 is couched between various interactions Jesus had with Gentiles. Looking back to Chapter 1, it is also important to remember that one of the key elements of Jesus' meals is inclusivity, inviting in and sharing company and food, with those who would not normally have been labelled as desirable dinner guests.

Cast your mind back to Chapter 2. What similarities and differences can you see between these two feeding miracles?

One such similarity is in their demonstration of Jesus' compassion and his desire to meet the needs of those around him. Yet even in this compassion some differences emerge. On this occasion it is Jesus who brings the people's needs to his disciples' attention. As in the previous feeding miracle Jesus desires the involvement of his disciples and Tom Wright notes that 'the closer we are to Jesus, the more likely it is that he will call us to share in his work of compassion, healing and feeding, bringing his kingdom-work to an ever wider circle.'[5] However, unlike in the feeding of the 5000, Jesus issues no overt command for the disciples to feed the people. Having experienced one feeding miracle already, perhaps Jesus was trying to develop their faith and see how much they had learnt from the previous encounter on the importance of relying on and trusting in him.

Looking at the scripture passages set for this chapter, do you think the disciples had applied what they had learnt about Jesus from the feeding of the 5000?

Despite the earlier feeding miracle, set in a similar wilderness environment, as well as having witnessed several other miracles in the meantime, the disciples do not appear to have grasped that it is Jesus' power and not their limitations that matter when it comes to solving problems. You could even argue that the location of this second feeding miracle encourages reliance on God further, as Jesus points out, in Mark 8 v 3, that he does not wish to 'send them home hungry' in case they 'faint along the way. For some of them have come a long distance'. This contrasts with the feeding of the 5000, where the disciples felt they could safely advise people to go away and buy some food. This time it is God or nothing. Yet the disciples' response remains one of incredulity at what Jesus is suggesting: 'How are we supposed to find enough food to feed them out here in the wilderness?' Again, they view the problem in terms of what they can or rather what they cannot achieve by their own efforts, overlooking the advice of passages such as Proverbs 3 v 5: 'Trust in the Lord with all your heart; do not depend on your own understanding.' When it came to the feeding of the 5000 and of the 4000, Jesus was asking them to do both instructions and one thing we can learn from the inclusion of both feeding miracles is how slow the disciples were at realising who Jesus was, what he was capable of and what it might mean for their own lives. This is not a problem unique to them and perhaps one reason for Mark and Matthew including both feeding miracles was to reassure early followers who were struggling with similar issues.

Re-read Matthew 16 v 1–4.

Who demands a miraculous sign from Jesus? What motive is given for this action?

Once more we have a feeding miracle which leads to a request for a sign, but in contrast to the feeding of the 5000, we are specifically told this time that it is the Pharisees and Sadducees who want a further sign from Jesus to validate his authority. As with the crowds' desire for a sign in the previous chapter, the motivation behind this request is impure. Prior to this point, Jesus' encounters with members from these two religious groups were frequently combative, as they tried to trip him up with knotty theological questions.[6] In light of this we can see that this demand for a sign is less likely to be born out of a desire to sincerely learn more about Jesus' ministry. Wright comments that Jesus 'would not perform signs to order'[7] and this refusal to do so is part of the reason Jesus was a challenging figure for his Jewish listeners, who found their expectations for the long-awaited Messiah frustrated. Yet this is foretold by Simeon, who tells Mary, 'This child is destined to cause many in Israel to fall, but he will be a joy to many others. He has been sent as a sign from God, but many will oppose him'[8] (Luke 2 v 34).

John Strohman refers to these Pharisees and Sadducees as 'sign-seekers'[9] and further writes that:

> They had seen the miracles before and chose not to believe. Even today it is a common attribute of sign seekers that they are never satisfied; they always want another sign, miracle, manifestation or experience.[10]

Here Strohman cautions readers against acting in a similar way, valuing the signs on their own terms as visual spectacles and not for what they point to. These miracles after all are not the final proof of Jesus' Messiahship, since the Bible warns that false prophets can perform them as well.[11] Furthermore, Jesus' aversion to delivering signs on demand, speaks also of his desire to only prove his identity as the Messiah in the way God had pre-planned. From Jesus' time in the desert where he was tempted for 40 days,[12] up until his crucifixion, there were many who tried to persuade Jesus to prove his identity in a way that conformed to the mould of a great human leader. Yet Jesus avoided all these traps, frequently leaving the area when his audience looked like they were going to make him king by force.[13]

How does Jesus respond to the Pharisees' and Sadducees' request? What does he accuse them of being?

In refusing their request, Jesus also exposes their spiritual blindness, pointing out that their ability to interpret signs only extends as far as the weather! Moreover, this insistence on a sign reinforces the division between Jesus and these religious groups, as Wright remarks that:

> Jesus seems to regard their request for a sign as being itself a kind of sign – a sign to him that 'this generation,' that is, the main stream of life and thought among his Jewish contemporaries, was determined not to hear the message he was announcing, determined to go their own way, to struggle for the kingdom on their own terms rather than his. He was staking his own vocation on the signs of God's kingdom that he was performing, and if they couldn't or wouldn't see it that must mean that their notion of the kingdom was radically different from his – and, if he was right, from God's as well.[14]

In Chapter 1 we began to look at what divided the Pharisees from Jesus and in this chapter's story we can once more see a clashing of kingdom visions. Whilst Jesus' vision of the kingdom promoted a servant's heart and sacrifice, the Pharisees through their adherence to the system of rules sought positions and privileges, for which Jesus takes them to task in Matthew 23. For example, in verse 4 of that chapter, Jesus says that the teachers of the law and the Pharisees 'crush people with unbearable religious demands', whilst in Matthew 11 v 30 Jesus proclaims that his 'yoke is easy' and his 'burden is light'. Again, in Matthew 23 v 6 the Pharisees are said to 'love to sit at the head table at banquets and in the seats of honour in the synagogues', whilst prior to the Last Supper we see the Messiah wash his disciples' feet. Given the opposing underlying priorities within each kingdom vision, Jesus' warning in Matthew 16 v 6 gains importance.

What does Jesus mean when he says, 'the only sign I will give them is the sign of the prophet Jonah' in verse 4?

This is not the first time Matthew has referred to this sign and it directly links back to the Old Testament story of the prophet

Jonah, which Matthew's Jewish audience would have been familiar with. Earlier in Matthew 12 v 39–40 Jesus confirms that the only sign he will give the religious teachers 'is the sign of the prophet Jonah'. He also adds that, 'for as Jonah was in the belly of the great fish for three days and three nights, so will the Son of Man be in the heart of the earth for three days and three nights.' This period of three days foreshadows Jesus' death and resurrection, which he more explicitly refers to in Matthew 16 v 21. However, in Matthew 12 we see Jesus also use Jonah's story to warn his audience of the dangers of turning down what God is now offering them, as in verse 41 Jesus tells them that 'the people of Nineveh will stand up against this generation on judgement day and condemn it, for they repented of their sins at the preaching of Jonah. Now someone greater than Jonah is here – but you refuse to repent.' This tone can also be heard in Matthew 16 v 4 when Jesus rebukes those demanding a sign from him.

Re-read Matthew 16 v 5–12.

What does Jesus mean when he tells his disciples in verse 6, 'Beware of the yeast of the Pharisees and Sadducees'? How do the disciples initially interpret his remark?

Unfortunately, the disciples have still not understood and begin to argue with each other about their lack of physical provision, despite having twice witnessed Jesus ensure there was enough food for everyone, on a grand scale. In Mark's account of this scene Jesus' response to their arguing, in verses 17–18, echoes the warning of Jeremiah 5 v 21[15]: 'Don't you know or understand even yet? Are your hearts too hard to take it in? You have eyes – can't you see? You have ears – can't you hear? Don't you remember anything at all?' Again, this reminds us that whilst Jesus' miracles were rooted in compassion and love, they were also demonstrations of who Jesus was, what he had come to do and the relationship he was offering. His words stress the need for his disciples to see this additional meaning and it is important that we do so too.

When Jesus talks about yeast in verse 6 he is not referring to it literally. The bread in the Passover meal was commanded by God to be unleavened, so over time leaven or yeast 'in rabbinic literature in a metaphorical sense' began to stand 'for sin or corruption'.[16] This is continued within the New Testament where it is used to represent 'false doctrine that permeates the churches and tries to corrupt it'[17] such as in Galatians 5 v 7–9, or hypocrisy as can be found in 1 Corinthians 5 v 4–8. The idea of 'false doctrine' takes us back to the idea of conflicting kingdom visions and Wright goes as far as to say that in this passage Jesus is putting the disciples 'on their guard against the wrong sort of kingdom vision'[18] which adulterates what Jesus was offering. This watering down of Jesus' kingdom vision comes in many formats including the syncretising of Roman practices by Herod and the Sadducees.

This focus on wrong priorities and working against Jesus' kingdom vision does not arise from nowhere, since prior to the feeding of the 4000, both Matthew 15 and Mark 7 lead up to the meal with Jesus' teachings on purity. Once more the Pharisees are shown to be wide of the mark, in rather blunt terms, such as in Matthew 15 v 13 where Jesus says, 'they are blind guides leading the blind, and if one blind person guides another, they will both fall into a ditch'. In Mark 7 the chapter begins with Jesus referring to the washing rituals the Pharisees highly valued and in verse 4 it says, 'this is but one of the many traditions they have clung to [...]' The phrase 'clung to' takes us forward to the Pharisees' demand for a sign from Jesus. This is not the first time they had asked him for one, nor would it be the last. Wrapped up with this request for a miracle are their tightly held ideas of what a Messiah should be like. You could say they 'clung to' these ideas too, so firmly that they were unable to let them go, in order to consider the new ideas Jesus' vision of God's kingdom was offering.

In addition, both Matthew's and Mark's accounts of Jesus' teachings on purity include Jesus' allusion to Isaiah 29 v 13: 'These people honour me with their lips, but their hearts are far from me. Their worship is a farce, for they teach man-made ideas as commands from God.' This accusation of duality, of only appearing moral on the outside, whilst being sinful on the inside, is one which Jesus makes many times. Within Jewish culture there were many rituals and activities used to prevent external defilement, which were used to demonstrate their membership of God's people and their separateness from Gentile culture. Yet as Jesus points out in Mark 7 v 20, when it comes to moral impurity, 'It is what comes from inside that defiles you.' This in turn brings us back to Jesus' warning concerning 'the yeast of the Pharisees and Sadducees'. Yeast, in order to make the bread rise, must work throughout the dough, yet in the case of the Pharisees' and Sadducees' alternative kingdom visions, this is not seen as a positive. Jesus' words urge his disciples not to entertain their ideas, which could pollute and mar their perception of Jesus' ministry and the vision of God's kingdom that he brings.

Take a look at Matthew 15 v 1–20 and/or Mark 7 v 1–23.

How do Jesus' purity teachings open the way for the Gentiles to be included into God's family?

Both passages flesh out Jesus' point that external rituals are meaningless if direct commandments from God are ignored, such as using the seemingly pious act of dedicating resources to God as a way of sidestepping the fifth commandment and the requirement to support parents in need. Jesus concludes this example by telling the Pharisees that this practice 'cancel[s] the word of God in order to hand down your own tradition'.[19] As well as revealing further divergence between Jesus and the Pharisaic kingdom vision, this example also highlights how external systems of rituals, used to indicate membership in God's family, are less important than a person's internal purity. This is a crucial step towards Gentiles being invited into God's community (without having to convert to Judaism) though the books of Acts and Galatians show this process was far from smooth. But at this early stage we can see the glimmer of truth that despite Gentiles not adhering to external Jewish rituals and customs, that did not mean they were barred from joining God's family. As later books of the New Testament show, it is faith in Jesus as our Saviour which makes you a member of God's family[20] and this acceptance, as we saw in Chapter 1 with Zacchaeus, enables and empowers believers to act in a way pleasing to God.

It is unlikely to be coincidental that following on from Jesus' teachings on purity and as he makes his way to Tyre, both Gospel writers include his encounter with a Gentile woman who discovers the house he is residing at. She begs him to heal her unwell daughter, calling him 'O Lord, Son of David' and she even 'worshipped him'. Yet as we read her story in Matthew 15 v 21–28, we see that whilst her petition is not immediately disregarded, by Jesus at least, it is not granted straight away either. She must be persistent. Ethnically she would have been perceived as outside of God's family and Jesus even brings this up in verse 26: 'It isn't right to take food from the children and throw it to the dogs.' Gentiles were often called 'dogs' at this time in Jewish culture in reference to their unclean state spiritually. Whilst modern readers may baulk at the term used, Jesus does not deny her spiritual condition and separation from God. Yet this line provokes rather than dismisses and we see the woman reply in verse 27, 'That's true, Lord, but even dogs are allowed to eat the scraps that fall beneath their master's table.' As Jesus says in verse 28, her 'faith is great', (in contrast to the disciples 'little faith'[21] at this point,) and it is because of this belief in who Jesus is and what he can do, that her request for a healing is granted rather than denied because she is not a Jew.

This interaction has been divisive for some, but I find it similar to the dialogue found in the feeding of the 5000, in which Jesus uses the conversation to generate internal wrestling within those he is speaking to. Why? For a pearl to be formed sand must enter an oyster and rub against the tissue inside. This rubbing causes irritation and it is this irritation which creates the hard substance we call a pearl. The same thing can happen when we wrestle and ruminate on the challenging questions and statements Jesus delivers. The more we grapple with them, the more our faith can become strengthened, and the Gentile woman went away with a lot more than an answer to her problem.

The NIV translates verse 26 as, 'It is not right to take the children's bread and toss it to the dogs.' This brings us back full circle to the feeding of the 4000. With the Gentile woman we see Jesus offering her the blessings and rights first intended for the Jews, and then in the miraculous meal we go from one Gentile person experiencing Jesus' grace, to a multitude. R. T. France argues that both feeding miracles are included in the Gospel of Matthew, as 'a deliberate intention to draw a parallel between Jesus' Jewish ministry and his ministry to Gentiles'[22] and that the feeding of the 4000 shows how the promises given in the former ministry were going to be extended to the latter.

Jesus and You

The questions below are there to help you consider your own walk with God and the themes raised in this chapter. These questions touch upon sensitive subjects, so remember to listen to each other's responses with consideration and care.

1. Chapter 3 has considered the responses that signs and miracles can elicit. Discuss in the group your own attitudes towards them, being respectful towards differing views and experiences. Has this been a difficult issue for you? How have your ideas developed or changed over time?

2. In the Bible passages looked at, Jesus also highlights how the Pharisees, those who were supposed to provide spiritual guidance, were themselves spiritually blind. This is a problem all believers are vulnerable to. Share with each other your ideas about how to deal with this difficulty. How can we find out where we are spiritually blind? How can we prevent this problem from taking over our spiritual perception?

3. Faith which has been stretched or challenged, is another theme we have explored. Charles Spurgeon wrote that: 'Untested faith may be real faith, but no doubt it will [...] likely remain stunted in its growth as long as it has no trials. Faith never prospers better than when everything comes against it [...] Testing is a learning experience [... and] faith solidifies through tribulations and grows in assurance and intensity the more it is exercised.'[23]

4. Do you agree with this statement? Is it something that you have experienced in your own life?

5. With both feeding miracles a demand for a sign has followed. Yet each time Jesus has exposed the impure motives lying beneath theses requests. Reflect within pairs, as a whole group or by yourself, on the common requests in your own prayer life and the motives which are fuelling them. Even if the request is for a 'good thing', are there any motives that need to be reconsidered?

Endnotes

1. John 10 v 9.
2. Hurtado, Larry (1989; 2011). *Understanding the Bible Commentary Series: Mark*. Michigan: Baker Books. p. 121.
3. The Decapolis 'is a geographical term referring to an area mostly south and east of the Sea of Galilee [...] The region in question was apparently constituted originally of ten Greek cities, nine of which were east of the Jordan River,

stretching from Damascus in the north to Philadelphia in the south. Later on, the Decapolis would include more than ten cities, but the original ten were, according to Pliny, Damascus, Philadelphia, Raphana, Scythopolis (the only city west of the Jordan), Gadara, Hippos, Dion, Pella, Gerasa and Canatha. Many of the cities of that region were founded after the death of Alexander the Great [...] In the second century B. C. E., a number of these Greek cities in the Decapolis fell to the Jews in the Maccabean revolution (168–64 B. C. E.). The cities were later liberated from Jewish dominance by the Roman leader Pompey [...]'

Anon. (1990). Decapolis. In: Mills, Watson E. *Mercer Dictionary of the Bible*. Georgia: Mercer University Press. p. 206.

4. See Mark 5 v 1–20.
5. Wright, T. (2001). *Mark for Everyone*. London: SPCK. p. 102.
6. See Matthew 12 v 13–27 and Matthew 22 v 23–46 for some examples.
7. Wright, T. (2002). *Matthew for Everyone: Part 2*. London: SPCK. p. 2.
8. This idea is similarly expressed by Paul in 1 Corinthians 1 v 22-23, when he is talking about the Good News: 'It is foolishness to the Jews, who ask for signs from heaven [...] So when we preach that Christ was crucified, the Jews are offended [...]'.
9. Strohman, J. (2012; 2015). *Application Commentary of the Gospel of Matthew*. San Diego: Cross Centred Press. p. 312.
10. *Ibid*, p. 314.
11. Jesus warns against such prophets in Matthew 24 v 24 and this theme also takes us back to Exodus 7 and 8, in which Pharaoh's magicians were able to duplicate the first two plagues God inflicted upon Egypt.
12. See Matthew 4 v 1–11, in which the Devil tries to get Jesus to misuse his power and authority and twice begins his

temptations with the phrase, 'If you are the Son of God...'

13. See John 6 v 15.

14. Wright, T. (2001). *Mark for Everyone*. London: SPCK. pp. 103–104.

15. 'Listen, you foolish and senseless people, with eyes that do not see and ears that do not hear.'

16. Ktav, S. (1987). *A Rabbinic Commentary on the New Testament: The Gospels of Matthew, Mark and Luke*. New Jersey: Publishing House Inc. p. 253.

17. Strohman, J. (2012; 2015). *Application Commentary of the Gospel of Matthew*. San Diego: Cross Centred Press. p. 315.

18. Wright, T. (2001). *Mark for Everyone*. London: SPCK. P. 104.

19. See Mark 7 v 13.

20. See Romans 3 v 28.

21. See Matthew 16 v 8.

22. France, R. T. (2007). *The New International Commentary on the New Testament: The Gospel of Matthew*. Michigan: William B Eerdmans Publishing Company. p. 600.

23. Spurgeon, C. (2008). November 12. In: Reimann, J. *Look Unto Me: The Devotions of Charles Spurgeon*. Michigan: Zondervan. p. 334.

Chapter 4

Party Invitations

The Parable of the Wedding Feast and the Parable of the Great Banquet

Do wedding guests mourn while celebrating with the groom?[1]

Parties and party guests all come in different shapes and sizes. Some prefer intimate dinners, with pre-set menus, whilst others love the roar of loud music and large crowds which battle for prime position at the all-you-can-eat buffet. Jesus participated in all kinds of parties, from a home cooked dinner with Zacchaeus (see Chapter 1), to the large meals found in the feeding of the 5000 and 4000 (see Chapters 2 and 3). In this chapter we are exploring the party that God has invited us all to. As mentioned in the introduction, both the Old and New Testaments use the image of a banquet or feast to symbolise God's invitation to accept his grace and become a part of his Kingdom on earth. The two parables we are looking at in this chapter consider God's invitation and who it is extended to, what is required of those attending and the reasons for, and the consequences of, turning it down.

It is important when examining these parables to remember that the banquet or feast is just an image to describe something which is bigger and more wonderful than we can possibly imagine. The image is given to help us get our heads around what God is offering, when he invites us into his restored kingdom, whilst knowing that right now our understanding can only ever be partial.[2] C. S. Lewis touches upon this in the final Narnia story, *The Last Battle* (1956), when the protagonists have made it into Aslan's country, and they begin to eat from the fruit trees. The narrator tries to describe what the fruit is like:

> Unfortunately no one can describe the taste. All I can say is that, compared with those fruits, the freshest grapefruit you've ever eaten was dull, and the juiciest orange was dry, and the most melting pear was hard and woody [...] If you had once eaten that fruit, all the nicest things in this world would taste like medicines after it [...] You can't find out what it is like unless you can get to that country and taste it for yourself.[3]

This passage presents us with three reflection points when contemplating the gift of God's invitation to us. The first is that language is limited in how fully it can describe what God's grace and kingdom are like. Secondly, only when we begin to experience the good things God wants to give us, can we see how the alternatives we are used to are infinitely inferior. Finally, and perhaps most importantly, in the way you can only know what a food is like by tasting it, you can only know what God's banquet is like by coming along and trying it for yourself.

Ice Breaker Questions
1. Have you ever turned up to an event in the wrong clothes?
2. What is your most common or your most creative excuse for getting out of doing something?

Key Scriptures to be Read
Matthew 22 v 1–14 (The Parable of the Wedding Feast)
Luke 14 v 7–24 (The Parable of the Great Banquet)

Both stories are parables, so who do you think is being represented by a) the host b) the guests who do not turn up

and c) the people who are found on the street and are invited to the banquet?

Since in this chapter we are looking at God's invitation to us, his role in these parables is understandably that of the host and his banquet is a symbol of God fulfilling his promises to Israel to make a new covenant with them. This new covenant is referred to in several Old Testament passages such as Jeremiah 31 v 31–34:

> 'The day is coming,' says the Lord, 'when I will make a new covenant with the people of Israel and Judah. This covenant will not be like the one I made with their ancestors when I took them by the hand and brought them out of the land of Egypt […] But this is the new covenant I will make with the people of Israel on that day […] I will put my instructions deep within them, and I will write them on their hearts. I will be their God, and they will be my people.'

Here God is promising a new way of life for Israel, a way which restores and renews their relationship with him. Jesus' arrival and ministry on earth was the start of these promises being completed and a key part of his work was to remind his listeners that God's gift to Israel was not for them alone, it was one they were supposed to share with the rest of the world.[4] Ultimately Jesus' message of salvation was also intended for those outside of Israel and this message included an invitation to become a part of God's family. Paul explores the new covenant's open membership and decries the nation-centric viewpoint in Romans 9 v 6–8:

> Well then, has God failed to fulfil his promise to Israel? No, for not all who are born into the nation of Israel are truly members of God's people! Being descendants of Abraham doesn't make them truly Abraham's children. For the Scriptures say, "Isaac

is the son through whom your descendants will be counted," though Abraham had other children, too. This means that Abraham's physical descendants are not necessarily children of God. Only the children of the promise are considered to be Abraham's children.

From this image of the new covenant, which invites everyone, regardless of their nationality or past, it is easy to witness God's mercy and grace, which is also echoed in the banqueting parable: The Lost Son.[5] In that tale the father kills the fattened calf to celebrate the return of his wayward son. Yet if we cast our minds back to the parables of the Wedding Feast and the Great Banquet, we see different aspects of God's character.

You might wish to briefly consider the differences between the father in the parable of the Lost Son, and the hosts we see in these parables.

The more negative emotions expressed through the hosts in these parables, have caused for some, difficulties in how they view God. This is an aspect we will be engaging with in more detail later in this chapter, exploring why this side of God is being shown.

In keeping with the elder brother in the parable of the Lost Son, the original guests in the parables of the Wedding Feast and the Great Banquet, who renege on their invitations, are interpreted as symbolising the Jewish people at the time. However, it is important to stress that these guests can be more specifically defined as anyone who chooses to reject God's invitation.

When it comes to social events, Roy Phillips notes that 'in [Ancient] Jewish culture, two invitations are sent out. The first asks the guests to attend, and the second announces that all is ready and provides the time at which the guests are to arrive.'[6] This structure is paralleled in the way God invites Israel into a new relationship with him, as the promises of the Old Testament are like the first invitation, and Jesus' ministry on earth, heralded by John the Baptist, is the second invite which lets everyone know that a new relationship with God is now available. Yet as Jesus showed in this parable and others, those who had accepted the first invitation were in danger of missing out on the 'party' of God's restored kingdom, by rejecting the invitation in its second format, i.e., Jesus himself.

As mentioned above Jesus' ministry extends to those outside of the Jewish community as well, and in the parables of the Wedding Feast and the Great Banquet, Gentiles are represented by the people who are found on the streets and are invited to the meal once the other guests have refused to come. In the parable of the Great Banquet these people are referred to as 'the poor, the crippled, the blind, and the lame', whilst the parable of the Wedding Feast refers to inviting the 'good and the bad, alike'. From these descriptions we can see that the hosts are willing to include those who would have been considered at the time as outcasts and as socially unacceptable. This group would have included not just Gentiles, but as Miroslav Volf notes:

> In the Palestine of Jesus' day, "sinners" were not simply "the wicked" who were therefore religiously bankrupt, but also social outcasts, people who practiced despised trades, Gentiles and Samaritans, those who failed to keep the Law as interpreted by a particular sect.[7]

Moreover, anyone within this group would have been regarded as 'unworthy of [...] participation in the community of God's people'.[8] Once more though, Jesus was keen to upset this established idea and the parable in Luke's Gospel particularly emphasises this with the teachings which come before this story.

Why would the people within this group be more grateful and

accepting of the banquet invite?

A poor person would naturally be more grateful for an invite to a banquet as they would more readily recognise and admit to their own lack of provision and their need for such sustenance. In the same way someone who is in a position where they can more easily recognise their own lack of righteousness, such as the tax collector Zacchaeus, can also perhaps be more willing to acknowledge their need for God's grace, which is a key facet of accepting God's invitation to be a part of his kingdom.

It is easy to merge these two parables together given the similar elements they contain.

What similarities can you identify?

At the heart of each parable there is an invitation by a host, an invitation which is rejected at least once.

How would you feel if you had organised a great party and then no one who was invited showed up?

The host in each parable is far from pleased and commands his servants to scour the neighbourhood to invite anyone they can find. In the parable of the Great Banquet the host, in verse 23, even tells his servants to look 'behind the hedges'; an instruction which recalls the dedicated nature of the shepherd in the later parable of the Lost Sheep.[9] In each instance the host of the party is determined to have a full house and both stories include a rejection of the guests who had originally been invited, but who decided not to come, though here we see one of the differences between these two stories.

Compare how the guests reject the host's invitation in each parable. How does the response of the host in each story differ?

R. T. Kendall notes that both texts reveal the 'danger of rejecting what God wants to do – and the danger of rejecting the Gospel'[10] though they express this point in different ways. Bible scholars, who have studied the chronology of the Gospels, such as Harold Hoehner, Stanley N. Gundry and Robert L. Thomas, place the parable of the Wedding Feast, as having been told during the Passion Week.[11] This was a week where the tension and animosity between Jesus and the religious authorities reached boiling point and led to Jesus' crucifixion. Just prior to this story Jesus also tells the parable of the Wicked Tenant Farmers. In this parable Jesus describes the way in which the tenant farmers rebel against the landowner of the vineyard they work on. They refuse to give the owner his share of the crop and they kill his servants one after another, until the owner sends his son. The tenant farmers kill him also, believing that they will possess the vineyard themselves if the rightful heir is dead. When Jesus asks the religious leaders what the landowner will do to those farmers, they say 'He will put the wicked men to a horrible death and lease the vineyard to others who will give him his share of the crop after each harvest.'[12] Yet it is those leaders who are represented by the tenant farmers, as they too have rebelled against God, the ultimate leader of their nation, and have violently ignored the messages he has sent through his prophets.

It is in light of this context we can examine the king's response in the parable of the Wedding Feast, as they have a similar message to share. As in the parable of the Wicked Tenant Farmers, the king's messengers are seized and killed by many of the guests originally invited to the feast. As discussed above, these guests are representative of those who were operating against the way in which God wanted to work and fulfil his promises to Israel and through them the entire world. This rejection of God's plan would extend to the crucifixion of his own son, which the parable of the Wicked Tenant Farmers foreshadows. The king's response equally mirrors that of the owner of the vineyard, and in verse 7 of the parable it says that the king 'was furious, and he sent out his army to destroy the murderers and burn their town'. Moreover, the king also completes the second part of the religious leaders' answer, as he sends his remaining servants to invite new guests to the banquet, who do attend.

Some have struggled with the violent outcomes of these parables, yet throughout the Gospels Jesus, with ever greater urgency, warns his listeners to turn away from the destructive path they are on; judgement is the only consequence of continuing along it. But it is not the consequence Jesus *wants* for anyone. G. B. Caird writes that 'for Jesus, Israel was at a cross-road; it must choose between two conceptions of its national destiny, and the time for choice was terrifyingly short'.[13] In Chapter 2 we explored how some Jews at the time were resistant to Jesus' message, as they did not agree with how God was working through Jesus to fulfil his promises to Israel. They had a different vision of what the Messiah would be like and how God's kingdom would be restored on earth. There was a popular hope for the Messiah to be a strong political and military figure who could defeat the Romans, and that God's kingdom would be restored with the restoration of Israel's land. This hope was fervently held by those such as the Zealots, a political movement which decided to take the restoration of Israel into its own hands. They were determined to rid Israel of Roman governance and their rebellion, fuelled by high tax rates and levels of income inequality, precipitated the First Jewish-Roman war (66–73 AD). Ignoring pleas from moderates to sue for peace, the Zealots pushed ahead with their own vision and in 70 AD Jerusalem and its temple were destroyed by the Romans. This event gains pertinence considering the parables' warnings and this is reinforced by Jon Isaak who suggests that:

The Matthean parable conclusions do not relay punishment for killing Jesus, but the consequences associated with persistent rebellion against God's intended purpose and enmeshment with narrow nationalistic ideals.[14]

Nevertheless, in these parables and elsewhere in the Gospels, Jesus continues to call upon 'Israel to renew its commitment to its founding narrative – to be both the blessed and *blessing* nation, the gathered and *gathering* nation, the saved and *saving* nation'.[15] Isaak sees the stark conclusions of these two parables as representing 'Matthew's conviction that Jesus's ministry involved reconstituting Israel in order that it might finally be what God had always intended it to be: namely, a "light to the nations."'[16] Furthermore, Isaak suggests interpreting the destructive language used in these parables, 'as the consistent result that flows from persistent rebellion against God's ways, whether by Jews or anyone else for that matter'.[17] He goes on to stress that:

> these consequences should not be characterised as a working out of God's vengeance [...], but illustrative of the way God honours even wilful rejection of life, which amounts to death.[18]

Jesus declares in John 14 v 6 he is 'the way, the truth and the life', so a rejection of God's invitation to eternal life through Jesus, is a rejection of life itself, and it is this that is then represented in the violent end of the original wedding feast guests.

Meanwhile, in Luke's Gospel with the parable of the Great Banquet, we find a different, though, still negative, response to the guests who did not attend. In this parable the guests who do not wish to attend, only offer excuses.

What distractions does the world offer to pull people away from accepting Jesus' invitation? Use the parable to give you some ideas but include suggestions of your own too.

Careers, possessions and relationships all crop up in the excuses proffered in the parable of the Great Banquet, and

the modern world has only added to that list. Returning to
C. S. Lewis' *The Last Battle*, we find another depiction of this
rejection of God's invitation. In Lewis' story it is a group of
dwarfs who refuse to be convinced by, and to understand, the
good things Aslan is giving them and his invitation to join him
in his country; to avoid being caught up in the destruction of
Narnia. Their rejection has many roots including self-interest,
the accompanying fear that another is getting something better
than they are, and their insistent belief that what is on offer is a
trick or a deception.

The host of the Great Banquet, whilst also 'furious', does not
destroy the original guests, as the king does in the parable of the
Wedding Feast. In the final verse of the parable the host instead
says, 'For none of those I first invited will get even the smallest
taste of my banquet.' Yet despite the lack of violent overtones,
the message is similar to that of the parable of the Wedding Feast:
those who refuse God's invitation cannot access the 'benefits' of
the party, namely, to be a part of God's restored kingdom on
earth and to be brought back into right relationship with him.
This brings us back to the point Isaak makes that 'God honours
even wilful rejection of life.' The denouement of this parable also
parallels the ending of the original Exodus story, in which most
of the Israelites intended to enter the promised land never did,
and the words of the host in verse 24 echo those said by God
in Numbers 14 v 30: 'You will not enter and occupy the land I
swore to give you.'

Gospel of Matthew and The Parable
of the Wedding Feast

**Looking at verses 11–14 of this parable, which guest is focused
upon and why? What does the host command should happen
to him?**

This is another aspect of the parable which has troubled some
readers, again because of its violent outcome. Yet Tom Wright

hits the nail on the head when he discusses this aspect of the parable:

> We want a nice story about God throwing the party open to everyone [...] We don't want to know about judgement on the wicked, or about demanding standards of holiness, or about weeping and gnashing of teeth.[19]

Wright goes on to remind us that 'moral choices matter'[20] and that 'the great deep mystery of God's forgiveness isn't the same as saying that whatever we do isn't really important because it'll all work out somehow.'[21]

It is often said that the host's judgement is too harsh for so minor an offence, the lack of wedding clothes. However, there are two important points to consider. The first one, is something every first-century Jewish listener would have known automatically, without having to be explicitly told in the story. When it came to weddings, especially those organised by a king or wealthy family, it was traditional in Jewish culture, for the host to provide a garment for all the wedding guests to wear. Dennis Nickel notes that this was done 'in honour of the groom and bride. To refuse the garment would be an insult to both the host and the groom. Either the host would think that the guest was arrogant and felt he did not need the clothes graciously provided or, even worse, was openly scorning the host and the groom'.[22] Knowing this, modern-day readers can see that the guest was not being penalised for lacking the finances to afford wedding clothes, since the host of the wedding was going to provide them. But this leads me on to the second important point, which is that since this story is a parable, the wedding guest's clothing is intended to be symbolic.

What do you think the wedding guest's clothes represent?

The answer to this question can be found in later passages of the New Testament. 'Jesus described his ministry as a wedding feast, with himself as the groom'[23] and this is explored more deeply in Revelation, in which John speaks of the marriage feast of the lamb, i.e., the final unification of Jesus with the Church. In chapter 19 v 7–9 of this letter it says:

'Let us be glad and rejoice, and let us give honour to him. For the time has come for the wedding feast of the Lamb, and his bride has prepared herself. She has been given the finest of pure white linen to wear.' For the fine linen represents the good deeds of God's holy people. And the angel said to me, 'Write this: Blessed are those who are invited to the wedding feast of the Lamb.' And he added, 'These are true words that come from God.'

In verse 8 it clearly states that the clothing of the bride, God's people, symbolises their 'good deeds' and this metaphor of clothing as either being moral or immoral behaviour, is one we can also use to understand the parable of the Wedding Feast. God's invitation to experience his grace and love is open to all, but the ending of the parable raises an important point: You cannot continue walking in sin and living your life as you did before, if you want to continue enjoying God's gift. This is an issue Paul returns to time and time again in his letters.[24] For example, most famously, in Ephesians 4 v 21–24 he writes that:

Since you have heard about Jesus and have learned the truth that comes from him, throw off your old sinful nature and your former way of life, which is corrupted by lust and deception. Instead, let the Spirit renew your thoughts and attitudes. Put on your new nature, created to be like God — truly righteous and holy.

The verbs 'throw off' and 'put on' embody this idea of our actions being like the act of putting on or removing clothing. After all the way we behave is just as visible as the clothing we wear and has even more to say about who we are as a person. Our actions must show God is a part of our lives and that his love is working in and through us. Wright puts it like this:

> God's kingdom is a kingdom in which love and justice and truth and mercy and holiness reign unhindered. They are the clothes you need to wear for the wedding. And if you refuse to put them on, you are saying you don't want to stay at the party.[25]

This again helps us to read the ending of the parable as an example of God honouring our decisions, even if one of them is to reject his invitation.

Yet it should be remembered that God's desire for us to leave our old way of living behind is motivated by love. Wright commenting on God's acceptance of sinful humanity, notes that: 'His love reached them where they were, but his love refused to let them stay as they were. Love wants the best for the beloved. Their lives transformed, healed, changed.'[26] This reminds us that God gave us Jesus and the Holy Spirit in order to help us to wear our 'wedding clothes' or to put it another way, to live our lives in a way pleasing to him. Several writers have powerfully explored this theme through allegories, including *Hinds' Feet on High* Places by Hannah Hurnard and C. S. Lewis' *The Great Divorce*.[27] It is important that both books acknowledge the difficulty in changing one's behaviour, as well as challenging the mental objections we might conjure up to put off having to change.

Gospel of Luke and the Parable of the Great Banquet

When Jesus is telling this parable, he is dining at the home of a Pharisee leader. But before telling this story he shares some advice on humility.

Re-read Luke 14 v 7–14.

How does Jesus turn social conventions upside down here? How do Jesus' teachings provide a lens for understanding the parable of the Great Banquet?

This passage is reminiscent of Jesus' meal with Zacchaeus, yet this time he is placing his listeners as the hosts who decide who is invited to the party. Jesus directly challenges the existing social convention of using 'banquets to flaunt and elevate one's status'.[28] It was customary, at the time, for hosts to 'invite friends of equal status and a few who were higher'.[29] The reason for this, was the anticipation of reciprocation, with the hosts then being invited to an even more socially exclusive party. Jesus' teachings overturn and frustrate this chain reaction, as the people he encourages his followers to invite and to accept, are those of little or no social credibility and who are in no position to reciprocate with an invitation of their own. Not only is Jesus redefining who is or is not important,[30] but he is also revealing how this decision to invite those outside of the social elite, mirrors God's own invitation to 'sinful human beings to dine at his banquet table of salvation'.[31] It is this theme which goes on to be examined more extensively in the parable of the Great Banquet.

Jesus' teachings at this meal also probe the motivations of his listeners, rooting out areas of self-interest. Here and in other places in the Gospels,[32] Jesus suggests to his followers that they can be motivated to do things to receive human praise, or to do the right thing, however painful it might be, because it is the action needed to show God's love in that situation.

Jesus and You

The questions below are there to help you consider your own walk with God and the themes raised in this chapter. These questions touch upon sensitive subjects, so remember to listen to each other's responses with consideration and care.

In looking at the parable of the Great Banquet, we have considered the excuses people may give for rejecting God's invitation. But we can also make excuses for not doing what God asks of us. Reflect individually, in pairs, or as a group, on whether there is something you have been putting off doing, which God has told you to do. What excuses are you using? How can you dismantle them?

In both parables there are servants who are called to search the area for people to invite to the meals. Invitation is the first step of evangelism. What do these parables suggest about this process? Is this something you feel you are incorporating into your own life?

Behaviour, and our commitment to acting in a way pleasing to God, in the parable of the Wedding Feast, is symbolised by the decision to wear the right clothes to the party. Again, reflect on whether there are any garments which you need to change in your own life. How might you go about doing this?

The parable of the Great Banquet is preceded by another story Jesus tells of guests all vying for the best seat at the feast. What do you feel the modern counterpart to this might be? Is this an area you have struggled in? Discuss with another what ways you could use to avoid falling into this trap.

Endnotes

1. Matthew 9 v 15.
2. Paul comments on this in 1 Corinthians 13 v 12: 'Now we see things imperfectly, like puzzling reflections in a mirror, but then we will see everything with perfect clarity. All that I know now is partial and incomplete, but then I will know everything and completely, just as God now knows me completely.'
3. Lewis, C. S. (1956; 1997). *The Last Battle*. London: Collins. pp. 129–130.

4. This intention is signposted from the very beginning with Abraham in Genesis. For instance, in Genesis 22 v 18 it says, 'And through your descendants all the nations of the earth will be blessed...'

5. See Luke 15 v 11–32.

6. Phillips, R. (2015). *The Kingdom According to Jesus: A Study of Jesus' Parables on the Kingdom of Heaven*. Indiana: WestBow Press. p. 73.

7. Volf, M. (1996). *Exclusion & Embrace: A Theological Exploration of Identity, Otherness, and Reconciliation*. Nashville: Abingdon Press. p. 72.

8. Nave, G. (2002). *The Role and Function of Repentance in Luke-Acts*. Boston: Society of Biblical Literature. p. 154.

9. See Matthew 18 v 12–14 and Luke 15 v 3–7.

10. Kendall, R. T. (2004). *The Parables of Jesus: A Guide to Understanding and Applying the Stories Jesus Told*. Michigan: Chosen Books. p. 232.

11. You can explore this idea further in Hoehner's *Chronological Aspects of the Life of Christ* (1977) and Thomas and Gundry's *A Harmony of the Gospels* (1978).

12. See Matthew 21 v 41.

13. Caird, G. B. (1994). *New Testament Theology*. Oxford: Clarendon Press. p. 361.

14. Isaak, J. (2011). *New Testament Theology: Extending the Table*. Oregon: Cascade Books. p. 129.

15. *Ibid*, p. 129.

16. *Ibid*, p. 129.

17. *Ibid*, p. 129.

18. *Ibid*, p. 129.

19. Wright, T. (2002). *Matthew for Everyone: Part 2*. London: SPCK. p. 82.

20. *Ibid*, p. 82.

21. *Ibid*, p. 83.

22. Nickel, D. (2014). *A Day in the Life of Jesus*. Georgia: TEACH

Services. p. 214.

23. Anon. (2008; 1996). The Messianic Banquet. In: *NLT Study Bible*. Illinois: Tyndale House Publishers. p. 1737.

24. Another key instance can be found in Colossians 3 v 5–10 and the apostle Peter also urges people to dress in humility in 1 Peter 5 v 5.

25. Wright, T. (2002). *Matthew for Everyone: Part 2*. London: SPCK. p. 85.

26. *Ibid*, p. 84.

27. A key example can be found in Chapter 11 of Lewis' book, in which a man wrestles with an Angel's offer to have a besetting sin, represented by a lizard on his shoulder, killed.

28. Anon. (2008; 1996). 14:12–13 Footnote. In: *NLT Study Bible*. Illinois: Tyndale House Publishers. p. 1737.

29. *Ibid*, p. 1738.

30. In Matthew 20 v 6, Jesus voices a similar idea when he says, 'So those who are last now will be first then, and those who are first will be last.'

31. Anon. (2008; 1996). 14:12–13 Footnote. In: *NLT Study Bible*. Illinois: Tyndale House Publishers. p. 1738.

32. See also Mark 6 v 1–4, in which Jesus instructs his followers to do their acts of kindness and charity privately.

Chapter 5

Set Apart

The Anointings of Jesus

But you are a chosen people, a royal priesthood, a holy nation, God's special possession, that you may declare the praises of him who called you out of darkness into his wonderful light.[1]

So far in this study we have seen meals used as vehicles for social change, as opportunities for sharing Jesus' radical kingdom vision, and as a means of demonstrating God's love and care for his people. They have also been occasions when Jesus' identity as the Messiah has been discussed, affirmed, or even challenged, and this chapter continues this theme, considering some of the meals during which Jesus was anointed.

Each of the Gospels includes an occasion when Jesus was anointed whilst dining at someone's house. The number of times Jesus was anointed on separate occasions is debated, with most arguments being put forward for either two or three times. Some suggest Matthew, Mark and John were writing about the same event, whilst others argue, based on differences[2] in the Gospel accounts, that there were three mealtime anointings, with only Mark and Matthew recording the same one. However, all three accounts show the increasing tension and the rising desire of the religious leaders to eliminate Jesus in the run up to the Passover celebrations, and Jesus' response to his disciples hinting at his forthcoming death. Multiple anointings of an individual, as a sign of honour and of someone's leadership being inaugurated and accepted by a community, has Old Testament precedents with David[3] being anointed three times and his son Solomon,[4] twice. So, the idea of someone having more than one anointing is not unheard of in the Bible. Of the four accounts, this chapter will be exploring the mealtime anointings recorded in the Gospels of Luke and John, considering their distinctive details, as well as looking at what these anointings teach us.

Ice Breaker Questions

1. Where have you felt the most welcome? What made that place so welcoming for you?
2. When people come to visit how do you make them feel most welcome? Does it depend on who they are?

Key Scriptures to be Read

Luke 7 v 36–50

John 12 v 1–8

If you are studying this as a group you may wish to just focus on one of the anointings, depending on the needs of your group and your time constraints.

What examples of anointing in the Bible can you remember? What purpose do you think these anointings had?

Anointing has early roots in the Old Testament, starting with Jacob in Genesis. God spoke to him through a dream at Bethel, and Jacob anointed the stone he had rested his head upon during the night.[5] Exodus and the remaining books in the Pentateuch,[6] reveal detailed instructions for the anointing of priests, sacrifices and the utensils used within the offerings made at the Tabernacle. Reverend John Brown notes that anointings can be done for varying reasons including 'to set apart [...and] to make ready'[7] people for joining God's family and/or an act of service for God. Considering this we can see anointing as a symbol of consecration. Freed from their slavery in Egypt, Moses tells the Israelites that they were: 'a people set apart as holy to God, your God. God, your God, chose you out of all the people on Earth for himself as a cherished, personal treasure'[8] and in a song sung by David, at the return of the Ark of the Covenant, Israel is named by God as his 'anointed ones'.[9] Both of these verses bring together the idea that whatever is holy is also set apart from that which is not, though we must remember from Jesus' time on earth, that set apart does not equate to refusing to engage with the rest of the world.

It took the life, death, and resurrection of Jesus to enable, on a larger scale, those outside of Israel to become a part of God's family, so it is not surprising that for such a role Jesus needed to be anointed as well. This chapter will be exploring these occasions, looking at what they have to say about Jesus' mission on earth, as well as our own actions. Brown suggests that Jesus' anointings were 'calling him to the office of Mediator, Prophet, Priest and King'[10] and both the Old and New Testaments refer to him as the 'anointed one'.[11]

After Jesus' resurrection and ascension, the book of Acts records the day of Pentecost, showing the anointing of his followers with the Holy Spirit. This anointing too set them, and those who have come after them, apart for God's service and community, with Paul writing in Ephesians that: 'When you believed, you were marked in him with a seal, the promised Holy Spirit.'[12]

The Gospel of Luke and the First Anointing

Looking at Luke chapter 7 as a whole, it is suggested that Jesus, and therefore Simon the Pharisee (whose house he is invited to dine at), were in the northern region of Galilee, in the area of Capernaum and Nain. This is taking into account that previously in this chapter, Jesus healed the slave of a Roman official in Capernaum and raised the Widow of Nain's son back to life. It is also important to note that in Luke 7 v 18–35, Jesus meets with John the Baptist's disciples, who have come from John to ask Jesus if he is the Messiah they've been expecting. This suggests that the anointing Luke is talking about here, took place two years prior to Jesus' death and resurrection, when John the Baptist was imprisoned, but still alive.

What does this passage tell us about the woman who anoints Jesus?

The specific details we have about this unnamed woman are few, but each shares an important part of her story and ours. At the very start of the account, we are told an 'immoral woman from that city' has come to see Jesus. Other translations refer to her as a 'sinner' and Matthew Black[13] has argued that in this description of the woman, wordplay occurs with the Aramaic word hayyābtā, which combines the meaning of sinner and debtor and can be found in earlier Jewish texts such as the *Isaiah Targum*.[14] The idea of sin constituting a form of debt is one Jesus explores more fully later during the meal, when he shares the parable of the two debtors to recast how the woman's actions were being perceived. Luke's narrative does not specify what the woman's sins were, though we know in verse 47, that 'they are many'. Yet it is this generality of her sins that makes it easier for us to identify with her situation of needing God's grace.

This account also strongly reveals an important quality within this woman: humility. The cleaning of guests' feet was a lowly job, done by someone at the bottom of the social hierarchy. It would not have been a pleasant task to perform, even with the proper equipment of water and a towel. Yet this woman did it with her own tears, kisses, hair and perfume, and vitally, for us, with such an attitude of gratitude and joy. Her gratefulness for what Jesus is offering to her, and her reverence for who he is (as shown by her kisses), is so immense that she does not take into consideration what others may think of her. Whilst today many societies do not see the need for women to conceal their hair, in the Jewish culture of the time, 'letting down her hair in public was scandalous, and could have constituted grounds for her husband to divorce her'.[15] This is corroborated by the reactions of some of the other dinner participants, who saw shame in her behaviour. Furthermore, Robert H. Gundry notes at this point in history:

> What others thought of you counted more than what you thought of yourself, so that there resulted what scholars call a dyadic personality, one determined largely by others rather than highly individualistic...[16]

Taking this concept into account, it is interesting to look not only at the woman's behaviour, but also Jesus' during his time on earth. Their actions suggest a steering away from this 'dyadic personality', and in other parts of the Gospels, Jesus frequently reminds his followers that the only personal (e)valuation worth holding on to is God's.

How does Jesus turn things upside down for Simon, when he challenges Jesus and the woman's behaviour?

In this study we have seen how Jesus' ministry has shaken up the status quo, as well as questioned the expectations many had about the arrival of the long-awaited Messiah. Tom Wright sums it up as 'a time of exuberant generosity, surprising grace, and at the same time fierce opposition which would meet God's judgement'[17] and he goes on to point out that this story in Luke's Gospel contains all these elements.

After the woman has anointed Jesus' feet, Simon is shocked to say the least. As a Pharisee and therefore a strict follower of Jewish teachings, Simon is likely to have believed that 'touching an unclean person polluted the one who touched'.[18] This connects back to the ideas we looked at in Chapter 1 when we explored the story of Zacchaeus, where Jesus was also judged for simply accepting a dinner invitation from a sinful man.

Simon was expecting Jesus to shun the woman, so when he does not, Simon can only conclude, in verse 39, that 'Jesus must not be aware of the true character of the woman [...] He concludes, then, that this Galilean preacher may not be a prophet after all.'[19] Yet Jesus overturns this incorrect assumption in several ways. Firstly, he demonstrates his disputed prophetic skills when he responds to Simon's mental criticisms. Next, he then provides a new framework for viewing the woman's actions, before shifting focus on to his host and his own conduct, which Jesus reveals as less than perfect.

As with his dinner at Zacchaeus', this is another occasion where Jesus uses a meal to confront and stand on its head the extreme 'keep your distance – don't touch'[20] and reputation-guarding policy of the culture he inhabited. To be set apart, is to live God's way, but that does not entail avoiding all those who do not. Moreover, Jesus' actions powerfully illustrate that 'the contagion of holiness overcomes the contagion of uncleanness'[21] as Walter Wink puts it.

How does Jesus regard the woman? And how does he show this through comparing her with his host?

This passage is worth comparing with Jesus' encounter with the Samaritan woman at the well,[22] as in both cases, in contrast to the dismissive attitudes of the other men around him, he accords his female interlocutors with dignity and respect. He does not ignore their sinful states, but neither does he overlook or look down upon them because of these sins or their gender.

Tom Wright comments that in Jesus' interactions with others 'human beings appear, not as society has "constructed" them, but as God sees them'[23] and this comes through on this occasion in the framework Jesus builds, to view not only the woman, but also his host. Hospitality was a crucial aspect of the culture and society Jesus lived in. It was in fact 'a matter of honour in ancient times'[24] and how successful your hospitality was, would affect how you were perceived by your community. In his comparison of these two people, Jesus identifies three ways that at the time marked you out as a good host: Providing water and a servant to wash your guests' feet, greeting them with a kiss and anointing their head with oil (to show honour towards a special guest). Yet as Jesus points out in verses 44–46, Simon, his host, did none of these things, whilst the woman in her own way did fulfil these criteria. Jesus is not simply trying to say that the woman is a better person, but he is trying to get his listeners to look at the motivations of the people they meet and to make them challenge the way they compare themselves to others. Perhaps the actions of others, such as the woman in this story, upset some social conventions; the people themselves may have little social standing, but Jesus suggests that this does not write them off as untouchable or of no value. In fact, their actions may be God's transformative love at work.

What is true faith shown as in this story?

In keeping with other stories and events in the Gospels, such as in the Parable of the Pharisee and the Tax Collector,[25] true faith is depicted as being bound up with how aware an individual is of their sinful state and of the enormity of God's grace in forgiving them. This awareness then leads to reversals in behaviour and often also an outpouring of love towards God and others. Jesus also uses a parable at this meal to stress this point, comparing two debtors who have had their debts cancelled. It is important to note that whilst Jesus says that 'a person who is forgiven little shows only little love' in verse 47, he is not suggesting that his followers commit many sins in order to improve their levels of love and gratitude! But this verse does perhaps intimate that those who view themselves as having only sinned a little and therefore only needing a little of God's grace, are firstly not realising the full extent of their sin, and also are implying on a level that they don't need God as much; an idea Jesus strongly challenges in his dialogues with those such as the Pharisees.

The Gospel of John and the Second Anointing

The second anointing of Jesus takes place in a very different setting. This time Jesus is with his close friends, Lazarus, Martha and Mary, and he is having dinner at their home in Bethany. Their friendship may not have very long roots, but they certainly ran deep. In Luke 10 we have the well-known occasion when Martha remonstrates with her sister for not helping her prepare the meal, and Jesus steps in to support Mary's desire to listen, at his feet, to his teachings instead. Then in John 11, Martha and Mary are far from uncomfortable in sharing how they feel when Jesus arrives four days after their brother Lazarus died. Neither of his sisters is afraid to show their pain and their hope that if he had come sooner Lazarus would be alive. This is a time of vulnerability for Jesus as he reveals his genuine sorrow over Lazarus' death, but it is also one of demonstrating God's power when Lazarus is brought back to life. This event is mentioned in John 12 when Jesus dines with these three, as it is noted that Lazarus was 'the man he had raised from the dead'.

What background tensions were surrounding this meal?

At the meal Mary anoints Jesus' feet with oil and it is said to take place six days before the Passover at which he was crucified, making the timing of this anointing highly significant. Just before this meal we learn the Pharisees and priests on the Jewish High Council are making plans to have Jesus killed, which then contrasts with how after his meal in Bethany we see Jesus' triumphal entry into Jerusalem where the crowds shout over him: 'Blessings on the one who comes in the name of the Lord! Hail to the King of Israel.'[26] Given this context Andreas Köstenberger writes that 'it is hard not to see royal overtones in Mary's anointing of Jesus.'[27] Wright, commenting on the mounting hostility to Jesus in the run up to the Passover, notes that:

> Passover was the setting Jesus chose for the final showdown with the Temple and its hierarchy, the final conflict (he believed) between the freedom movement he had been spear heading and the new Pharaohs, the forces both of pagan rule and of Temple misrule. He had been acting, up until now, somewhat like Moses, doing striking things which functioned as signs of the coming freedom. Now it was time to confront the Red Sea itself.[28]

When looking at this meal in Bethany it is important to remember these background tensions, as they emphasise the tenderness and care of Mary's anointing, which also set Jesus apart and prepared him for the next monumental part of his ministry; namely that of becoming the final and ultimate Passover sacrifice.

Can you think of any examples from your own life or from the news of extravagant generosity? What is your reaction to such moments?

When it comes to Mary's extravagant act of pouring a 12oz jar of expensive perfume over Jesus' feet, and then wiping those feet with her own hair, there was at least one guest at the dinner who was not happy about this. Judas Iscariot complains that it was a waste, that the perfume should have been used by selling it and then giving the money to the poor. A noble gesture surely?

If you were in this scene, who would you naturally side with? What do you think was motivating Mary's and Judas' differing actions?

To return to an idea we explored in the first anointing of Jesus, it is essential to consider the motives at work. John 12 v 6 undermines the potentially pious motive behind Judas' words, as John informs us that Judas was a 'thief, and since he was in charge of the disciples' money, he often stole some for himself'.

In contrast we have Mary at Jesus' feet, a place she has been before, but perhaps she is now acting upon what she has learnt from him. Like the sinful woman in the anointing Luke records, Mary's position is one of humility, and corrects any misconceptions that she might be workshy or unprepared to do menial tasks. Yet in some ways Mary's anointing of Jesus' feet is less about herself and the forgiveness she has received and is more concerned with Jesus himself and what lies ahead for him, namely his death and burial. Remembering the 'royal overtones' of this anointing, it is fitting that it was common practice, in the Old Testament and during Jesus' time, for kings to be buried with perfumed ointments. This is another sign pointing towards Jesus' kingship.

When Jesus defends Mary in verse 8 saying to his disciples that 'you will always have the poor among you, but you will not always have me', he is not being self-centred, nor is he instructing them to *never* help the poor. He is in fact echoing Deuteronomy 15 v 11 which states that: 'There will always be some in the land who are poor. *That is why I am commanding you to share freely with the poor and with other Israelites in need.'* Helping those in need is not an optional extra. Instead, Jesus is trying to make his followers realise that the current way they are experiencing him won't stay the same forever. They are a part of a very special moment in history and at this dinner it is a matter of days before everything they are used to will be thoroughly changed and shaken up.

Where else in the Gospels does Jesus try to intimate to his disciples that they won't have him around in the same way for ever?

From very early on in his ministry Jesus alludes to, or directly mentions that a time is coming when he will not be with his disciples as he is now. An important example[29] can be found in Mark 2 when John the Baptist's disciples criticise Jesus' followers for not fasting and Jesus issues this rhetorical question in verse 19: 'Do wedding guests fast while celebrating with the groom?' He goes on to answer his own question saying, 'Of course not. They can't fast while the groom is with them. But someday the groom will be taken away from them, and then they will fast.' This example particularly brings out the idea that Jesus' time on earth was unique, special, and was going to entail doing new things for a time, which brings us back to Mary's actions at this meal. Her act of generosity was fitting for a specific moment, and it was not disregarding the wider teachings around helping the poor. Charles Spurgeon, in a rhetorical question of his own, asked: 'Is anything wasted which is all for Jesus? It might rather seem as if all would be wasted which was not given to him.' Letting Jesus use our resources, his way, is the important point here. What Mary's extravagant gesture encourages us to do, is not to stop supporting those in need in the usual ways, but to be open to helping others generously, using methods or actions that might at a first glance seem ridiculous, crazy or wasteful, yet will actually go on to make a difference in their lives in a way we might never have imagined or predicted.

Jesus and You

The questions below are there to help you consider your own walk with God and the themes raised in this chapter. These questions touch upon sensitive subjects, so remember to listen to each other's responses with consideration and care.

1. Have you ever decided to not do something because you feared what others might think of you? How did you feel afterwards? What other factors hold you back from doing the things you should?
2. Humility and generosity are two values at the forefront

of these meals in which Jesus is anointed. Reflect upon your own life. How much do these qualities influence your actions, words and perception of others? How can you incorporate these into your life more?

3. You may wish to ask a close friend or family member how they perceive these traits in you.

4. A key facet of being anointed, as a Christian, is being set apart for a particular service for God. What do you think this service might be for you?

5. You can consider this in terms of all Christians generally, or more specifically for your own life and context.

6. Consider how much Jesus has forgiven you for. How good are you at being grateful and expressing your love to God for this daily act of mercy? How can you develop this attitude in your life more?

Endnotes

1. 1 Peter 2 v 9.

2. These differences include where the meals took place, as well as who was anointing Jesus and where on his body. These differences for some suggest that Matthew and Mark were writing about a slightly later event than the one John speaks of.

3. See 1 Samuel 16 v 12–13, 2 Samuel 2 v 4 and 2 Samuel 5 v 3.

4. See 1 Chronicles 23 v 1, 1 Kings 1 v 39 and 1 Chronicles 29 v 22.

5. See Genesis 28 v 18.

6. This is the name given to the first five books of the Old Testament.

7. Brown, Rev J. (1833). *A Dictionary of the Holy Bible*. New York: J & J Harper. p. 53.

8. See Deuteronomy 7 v 6. This citation is from the Message translation.

9. See 1 Chronicles 16 v 22. This citation is from the Message

translation.

10. Brown, Rev J. (1833). *A Dictionary of the Holy Bible*. New York: J & J Harper. p. 53. The four roles mentioned are also ones taken up by various people mentioned in the Old Testament. For example, Aaron was anointed for his role as a priest and Moses was anointed by the Holy Spirit in Numbers 11 v 17–25, for his service as a mediator between Israel and God. Prophets such as Jeremiah were also anointed and set apart for their service to God, (see Jeremiah 1 v 5), and of course Israel's kings were anointed such as David and Solomon.

11. Jesus in Luke 4 explicitly sees himself as being prophesied about in Isaiah 61 v 1 and that his ministry was a fulfilment of it. This verse details what the 'anointed one' has been sent by God to do. See also Psalm 2 v 2, Daniel 9 v 25–26 and Isaiah 10 v 27 for other OT references. The name 'Christ' is derived from the word *chrīstós*, which is Greek for anointed one. This Greek word is used to translate the Hebrew word *Mašíaḥ*, the Messiah. There are many references from the NT using this phrase including John 1 v 41, Acts 9 v 22 and Acts 17 v 2–3.

12. See Ephesians 1 v 13.

13. Black, M. (1967). *An Aramaic Approach to the Gospels and Acts*. Oxford: Clarendon. p. 181–183.

14. The Jewish scriptures, also known as the Tanakh, over time developed oral translations and interpretations, given by teachers in a language their audience could understand if they were not conversant in Hebrew. Such translations became increasingly relevant, since as the first century BC came to a close, Aramaic was more frequently used than Hebrew. They were known as the targumim, with an individual translation being a targum. Eventually they were written down.

15. Anon. (2008; 1996). 7:38 Footnote. In: NLT Study Bible. Illinois: Tyndale House Publishers. p. 1719.

16. Gundry, Robert H. (2012;1970). *A Survey of the New Testament.* 5th ed. Michigan: Zondervan. p. 57.

17. Wright, T. (2001). *Luke for Everyone.* London: SPCK. p. 91.

18. Yancy, P. (2009). January 14th Undesirables. In: *Grace Notes: Daily Readings with a Fellow Pilgrim.* Michigan: Zondervan. p. 34.

19. Evans, Craig A (2011;1990). *Understanding the Bible Commentary Series: Luke.* Michigan: Zondervan. p. 122.

20. Posterski, D. (2013). *Jesus on Justice: Living Lives of Compassion and Conviction.* Ontario: World Vision Canada.

21. Wink, Walter (1992; 2017). *Engaging the Powers: 25th Anniversary Edition.* Minneapolis: Fortress Press. p. 140.

22. See John 4 v 4–42.

23. Wright, T. (2001). *Luke for Everyone.* London: SPCK. p. 92.

24. Anon. (2013). Hospitality. In: Longman III, Tremper *The Baker Illustrated Dictionary.* Michigan: Baker Books. p. 710.

25. See Luke 18 v 9–14.

26. See John 12 v 13.

27. Köstenberger, A. (2004). *John.* Michigan: Barker Academic. p. 361.

28. Wright, T. (2001). Mark for Everyone. London: SPCK. p. 189.

29. Jesus also foretells his own death and time of suffering in passages such as Mark 8 v 31–33, when he and his followers are in the area of Caesarea Philippi and Peter declares that Jesus must be the Messiah.

Chapter 6

God's Kingdom Vision

Jesus and The Last Supper

The cup of blessing that we bless, is it not a participation in the blood of Christ? The bread that we break, is it not a participation in the body of Christ?[1]

To commemorate God rescuing the Israelites from Egyptian slavery, the Passover season and in particular the Passover Seder[2] was established. Yet this meal was not intended to solely celebrate what was done in the past to spare the Israelites from slavery and the death of their firstborn children. It was also designed to look forward to the future when humanity would be saved from sin and death itself. This was a meal which anticipated what would take place hundreds of years later when Jesus laid down his life to atone for our wrongdoings. At the Last Supper Jesus, outlines how this meal was all along a signpost to himself and the sacrifice he was about to make on behalf of humankind. This is a message which Christians still proclaim today when they take part in communion and Paul in 1 Corinthians reinforces this point: 'For every time you eat this bread and drink this cup, you are announcing the Lord's death until he comes again' (11 v 26).

Beginning with the first Passover feast in Exodus, this chapter will be exploring the common ground between that meal and the Last Supper. In doing so the aim is to dig further into understanding how the symbolism of the Passover meal foreshadows and anticipates Jesus' sacrifice on the cross, as well as how that offering enabled God's new covenant with humanity. Deuteronomy 16 v 16 states the annual requirement for every Israelite man[3] to make a pilgrimage to Jerusalem, to celebrate the Festival of Unleavened Bread, the Festival of First Fruits, and the Festival of Shelters. In each case these festivals were opportunities to deepen one's relationship with God and be reminded of important truths about God's relationship with his people. Finally, this session will also be discussing the intermingling of betrayal with Jesus' kingdom vision, which he provides further teaching on during the Last Supper. This vision not only considers the new relationship between God and man, but also the way humans should interact with each other.

You may also wish to read or re-read the information provided in the Introduction concerning the Passover season and meal.

Ice Breaker Questions

1. How can actions be more powerful than words?
2. What events do you consistently commemorate? How do you celebrate or remember them? (This can be personal or national events.)

Key Scriptures to be Read

Exodus 12 v 1–30
Matthew 26 v 17–35
Luke 22 v 24–27
John 13 v 3–17 and 31–35

What foods are eaten during the Passover meal? What were they intended to represent?

The centrepiece of the Passover meal is the year-old male lamb or kid, which crucially had to have no defects. To understand what the lamb represents we have to look at one of the main purposes of this meal as a whole, which was atonement. The Israelites, as a community, had spent hundreds of years living in Egypt before their exodus. They were quite literally separated from the land God had promised them through Abraham and during that time they had also become separated from God at a deeper spiritual level. They did not see themselves as God's chosen people, nor did they really know what it meant to live like one. The Passover meal before their flight from Egypt was God's first step in correcting this situation.

Prior to this meal God had sent nine plagues to Egypt, but we are often told how these plagues did not affect the Israelites or their animals. Yet this final plague, the death of all firstborn sons, was different. This was a plague they were not automatically exempt from, as they had to make an atonement by smearing blood from their sacrificed lamb upon their doorposts. The NLT when considering the reason for this, notes that:

> Death reigns in the world because of sin, and in light of God's justice, sin cannot be ignored; it must be either punished or atoned for. Since blood represents life[4] [...] it alone is acceptable for the forgiveness of sins.[5]

Michael Cogen further points out how 'atonement requires a reparation, payment, or ransom to the offended party'[6] who in this case is God. Yet God, perhaps surprisingly to us, then goes on to provide the means for that payment, in order to have his relationship with us repaired. In Exodus that payment was the unblemished lamb, which freed the Israelites from their slavery in Egypt and ended their separation from God. Jesus was God's final provision of an atonement payment. Like the lamb with no defects, Jesus had no sin, and his sacrifice frees all those who accept it, from sin and death; a role John the Baptist saw in him from the very start of Jesus' earthly ministry: 'Look! The Lamb of God who takes away the sin of the world!'[7] The lengths God will go to, to restore his relationship with us, are breathtaking, considering that God did not cause the separation in the first place. Not only do the Israelites, and now us, see who we are in the Passover meal, but we also clearly see God's character which exudes compassion, yet not in such a way that justice is compromised.

Exodus 12 also provides several instructions concerning the bread for the meal, which is to be made without yeast. For this first Passover meal it was especially practical as the Israelites were going to be departing from Egypt in such haste that there would be no time for preparing the bread in the usual way. Yet this bread without yeast was also symbolic. Richard Booker explains that 'leaven became symbolic of the Hebrew's old life of bondage in Egypt under Pharaoh and the Egyptian's world system. Unleavened bread symbolised their putting off this old life as they came out of Egypt'[8] a theme we explored in Chapter 3.

A final component of the meal, mentioned in Exodus 12, is the bitter salad greens, which could have been comprised of plants such as 'lettuce, endive, parsley, watercress, cucumber and horseradish, all of which were   plentiful in areas of the Sinai Peninsula, Palestine, and Egypt'.[9] The word 'bitter' used in chapter 12 takes us back to the very beginning of Exodus, as in 1 v 14 we are told that the Egyptians 'made their lives bitter, forcing them to mix mortar and make bricks and do all the work in the fields'. Eating the bitter greens was a memory aid for the Israelites to remember how hard it was living in Egypt, separated from God. Life was not going to be problem-free for the Israelites in the wilderness, but it would bring the joy of freedom and reconciliation.

If you are using this study guide in a group context it is recommended that you split participants into two groups for this next question. One group should read Exodus 12 v 1–14 and Matthew 26 v 17–35. The second group should read Exodus 12 v 1–30, Exodus 12 v 46 and John 19 v 28–37. Each group needs to compare the passage(s) in Exodus concerning the Passover meal with their New Testament reading, which either covers the Last Supper or Jesus' death. What parallels and differences can be drawn? Consider the purpose of the Passover meal and

what Jesus was trying to do through it.

None of the accounts of the Last Supper mention all the rituals contained in a typical Jewish Passover meal, (which had become more ceremonially elaborate by Jesus' day). Instead, attention is drawn to the bread and the wine. After all, the focus for the Gospel writers was how the Passover meal foreshadowed Jesus' sacrifice on the cross. In Matthew 26 v 26–28, we see Jesus draw upon himself, through the bread and the wine, the full purpose of what the Passover was intended to do, and this is something Jesus also speaks of after the feeding of the 5000 in John 6 v 53–54,[10] which we looked at in Chapter 2. In those verses, Jesus declares that 'anyone who eats my flesh and drinks my blood has eternal life' which situates him within the role of the Passover lamb. Brant Pitre writes that:

> Jesus knew full well what any first-century Jew would have known: when it came to the Passover, you did not only have to kill the lamb; in order to fulfil God's law, in order to be saved from death, you had to eat the lamb.[11]

Whilst Jesus is not advocating cannibalism, his words in John 6 and during the Last Supper emphasise how his death and resurrection, must be wholeheartedly accepted and made a part of each believer's life. This idea is returned to time and time again in Paul's letters such as in Galatians 2 v 20: 'My old self has been crucified with Christ. It is no longer I who live, but Christ lives in me. So I live in this earthly body by trusting in the Son of God, who loved me and gave himself for me.'

Although wine is not specifically mentioned in the first Passover, 'wine in Judaism symbolises the life force – vitality, the joy of living'[12] and therefore over time became a traditional component of festivals and times of celebration. Wine was therefore associated with joy and happiness. The Passover meal was no exception to this trend, as it went on to incorporate four servings of wine, which many Jewish teachers believe relate to 'the four different expressions of divine deliverance used in the Torah in relation to the redemption of Israel'.[13] So the wine in this instance becomes intertwined with ideas of freedom and liberation, which chimes in with many of the promises God makes to Israel in Exodus.[14] As mentioned above the Passover meal is focused on atonement, in which a life is sacrificed on behalf of another and this too finds its echo in the wine and in Jesus' words at the Last Supper, 'Each of you drink from it, for this is my blood, which confirms the covenant between God and his people. It is poured out as a sacrifice to forgive the sins of many.' The wine takes us back to the Passover lambs and the blood they shed, and how this time Jesus was going to submit to the same process. The important difference though is that Jesus only needed to undergo this ordeal once, ending the need for annual sacrifices.

Whilst the Gospel accounts of the Last Supper attest to the disciples going on ahead to prepare the Passover meal, the Passover lamb itself is not specifically mentioned. Yet in Jesus' discourse on the meaning of the bread and the wine, the ultimate, long foretold,[15] Passover lamb emerges. Jesus was to be the final sacrificial lamb. Moreover, as we compare the preparations for the traditional Passover lamb, we can see a number of parallels between them and the manner in which Jesus died. We have already mentioned that Jesus had no defects, like the original Passover lamb and also like those lambs Jesus died on the cross at 3pm; the time the Passover lambs were killed. Furthermore, in Exodus 12 v 46 the Israelites are instructed not to break any of the lamb's bones, which is mirrored in John 19 v 33, detailing how the soldiers did not need to break Jesus' legs to hurry on his death, as he was already dead. Even the manner of how the Passover lamb was cooked is paralleled. Exodus 12 v 9 forbids the lamb to be eaten raw or boiled, the whole lamb had to be roasted, which Richard Booker notes would have entailed putting the lamb 'on a spit shaped like a crossbar, so that its body could be spread open'[16;] a position remarkably like Jesus' on the cross.

When it comes to the various instructions for sacrifices in the Old Testament,[17] a key command is for the blood of the animal to be drained from its body, and in Rabbinical teachings such as those found in the Mishnah Tamid 4.2, it is specifically mentioned that the blood be drained from the heart. John's account of Jesus' death once more reveals a similarity with the Passover lambs, as when the soldier in 19 v 34 sticks his spear into Jesus' side, blood and water flows out. The NLT suggests it is likely that the soldier's spear 'punctuated Jesus' pericardium sac around the heart, releasing these fluids'.[18]

Jesus' blood was not literally sprinkled around anyone's home the way the lamb's blood in Exodus was, an action performed to ensure God's judgement would pass over the Israelite households. Nevertheless, Jesus is identified by Paul as 'our Passover [...] sacrificed for us' in 1 Corinthians 5 v 7, and disciples Peter[19] and John,[20] in their letters, see Jesus' shed blood as the means to us being redeemed and cleansed from sin. Returning to the instructions of Exodus, Richard Booker symbolically describes this as 'when we apply' Jesus' blood 'to the doorpost of our heart, death cannot hold us'.[21] Similarly in the way the lamb's blood created a protective seal over the Israelite households at the first Passover, in Ephesians 1 v 13 we are told that through believing in Jesus we have been 'marked with a seal, the promised Holy Spirit'. Again, this is a sealing which ensures our transgressions have been forgiven and already atoned for on the cross.

The Passover: Forging a New Relationship
What is a covenant? In the Old Testament, what covenants did God make and with whom?

The very nature of a covenant reveals God to be personal and relational, as such an action involves two parties agreeing on a binding contract. This agreement itemises what each side needs to do to maintain the covenant and during the ratification process promises from both parties are made. A sacrifice would often occur too, part of which would be eaten in a meal afterwards, which reminds us of the covenantal dynamic of meals at this time and why Jesus' decision in the Gospels to dine with ceremonially unclean people was so controversial. The Old Testament includes many examples of God making covenants with individuals and groups, before and after the Exodus of the Israelites, such as with Noah and David. However, this study will be focusing on the one God made with Abraham. At several points in Genesis such as in chapters 15 and 17, God reaffirms his promise to give Abraham a multitude of descendants and the promised land in Canaan. Abraham is also reminded of his own and his descendants' responsibilities, including carrying a mark of the covenant on their bodies through the act of circumcision. Yet this covenant was not made between two equals. Usually, 'the sign of ancient covenants often involved the cutting in half of animals, so that the pledging parties could walk between them, affirming that the same should happen to them if they broke the covenant'[22] and in Genesis 15 such a corridor of animals is produced. However, given our fallen nature there is no way Abraham or his descendants could keep their side of the bargain. Sin gets in the way. At one time or another it is likely that we have experienced a friendship or relationship which has been broken. Some of these have been repaired, but many are not, and the damage caused can be deeply painful. Nevertheless, God, despite experiencing this problem countless times, was determined to repair his relationship with Israel and the world. Even when he made his covenant with Abraham, he foresaw this difficulty and in verse 17 we read that only God walked between the halved meat. Doug Hershey regards this as God showing that 'He will be the one to establish, accomplish, and confirm this covenant [... which] means the total and complete success of the covenant would not depend on Abram but on God, and it would last until the end of time.'[23] God's grace in doing this is mind-blowing in its generosity and compassion and is an important point to bear in mind as we switch our attention to the new covenant God wanted to make.

On several occasions the Old Testament prophets such as Jeremiah and Ezekiel speak of God bringing in a new covenant between himself and his people.

How was the new covenant meant to be different from the existing one? What was Jesus' role in this new covenant?

You may wish to look up the following Bible passages: Jeremiah 31:31–34, Ezekiel 26:24–27, 37:1–14 and Hebrews 9.

The passages from Jeremiah and Ezekiel emphasise how the new covenant will resolve the limitations of the existing agreement, in particular the issue 'that it lacked the power to enable people to do what it commanded'.[24] Paul brings up this problem in Romans 8 v 3, 'The law of Moses was unable to save us because of the weakness of our sinful nature.' In contrast to the externally written down laws of Moses, the new covenant operates internally within each believer. God declares this idea himself in Jeremiah 31 v 33, when he says, 'I will put my instructions deep within them, and I will write them on their hearts.' Moreover, in Ezekiel 36 v 25–27, God further says that in his new covenant:

I will sprinkle clean water on you, and you will be clean, your filth will be washed away, and you will no longer worship idols. And I will give you a new heart, and I will put a new spirit in you. I will take out your stony, stubborn heart and give you a tender, responsive heart. And I will put my Spirit in you so that you will follow my decrees and be careful to obey my regulations.

This indicates how the new covenant envisages improving upon the existing one, as it empowers God's people to know and access him in a new way, through the Spirit, that will help them to follow his commands in a way they could not do before.

This brings us back to Jesus and the Last Supper in which he tells his disciples that the cup of wine they are about to partake in is a sign of 'the new covenant between God and his people — an agreement confirmed with my blood, which is poured out as a sacrifice for you'.[25] Once again God is not relying on us to ensure the covenant is fully kept. Instead, Jesus takes on the role of mediator and guarantor for the agreement.[26] It is through Jesus' shed blood that the new covenant is inaugurated, in the same way that the sacrifices made by Moses authenticated God's agreement with Israel.[27] Hebrews 10 v 1 sums it up well when it says, 'the old system under the law of Moses was only a shadow, a dim preview of the good things to come, not the good things themselves.' This is a helpful lens through which to see the Last Supper. It was not just another Passover meal, nor was Jesus simply trying to put a new spin on it. He was in fact re-framing the meal itself. The Passover was the copy or imitation of what was to come, Jesus' death on the cross and his resurrection.

The Passover: Betrayal

Looking at Matthew 26 v 17–35, who betrays or is predicted to betray Jesus? How do these betrayals differ? What are the motivations behind them?

It seems ironic, though unsurprising given humanity's fallen nature, that during a meal in which a new, better, and closer relationship with God is being announced and established, betrayal would rear its ugly head. Tom Wright sees 'the blend of celebration and betrayal in the scene at supper [...as] preparing us for the blend of triumph and tragedy in the crucifixion itself'.[28] Betrayal is the very opposite of relationship and can catastrophically derail connection. It can also be deeply painful and take a long time to heal, especially if the betrayer was close to you.

Jesus mentions Judas' betrayal in verse 23, which is made all the starker by the fact that all the disciples had shared food from the same bowl as Jesus. This was a social custom of the time that reinforced the fellowship and trust aspect of meals. In Matthew's account the change in relationship is depicted in subtle word differences. Judas refers to Jesus as 'Rabbi' whilst the others use the word 'Lord'. Both are respectful terms, yet they describe quite different relationships. The Greek word *kurios* is often deployed in the New Testament to speak of God, and in English it is translated as the word 'Lord'. It's a word denoting authority and Judas' reluctance to use this name for Jesus is telling. If Jesus is just a good teacher to you, he can have a profound influence on your life and the choices you make, but his reach will have boundaries and limitations. You can take or leave what he has to say. Yet if Jesus is your Lord, then the relationship is very different. By receiving Jesus into your life in that role, you are not only allowing him complete and total access to yourself, but you are also accepting his rule within all parts of your life. Judas' actions after this meal go on to show decisively that he does not want Jesus to have authority in his life and his betrayal is a form of rebellion.

Peter's betrayal, which is also predicted in this passage, seems to partially come from different motives. His words express intense devotion, such as in verses 33 and 34, in which he promises he will not abandon Jesus. His discrediting of Jesus' prophecy that he will be deserted by his followers, recalls his denunciation of Jesus' foretelling his own death in Matthew 16 v 21–23. In a way you could say in these moments Peter thinks he knows best, or rather better than Jesus. This kind of intellectual pride on the surface may appear to be well meant. After all it is not unkind of Peter to want Jesus not to die, or for him to be determined to stand by Jesus. But if we look deeper, beneath the good intentions, there is arguably still a resistance to Jesus' authority. Peter wants things to happen his way, not Jesus' way, and Jesus pulls him up on that in Matthew 16 v 23, 'You are seeing things merely from a human point of view, not from God's.' Equally when we are resistant to Jesus' authority, we are likely to be working in our own strength, which we know has limitations. Peter finds this out soon after Jesus is arrested and he is unable to resist the temptation to deny knowing him three times, as Jesus predicted he would. The final chapter in this study will be exploring how Jesus restores this relationship.

The Passover: The Kingdom Vision

Yet betrayal, however close to home, did not stop Jesus in his mission to bring God's kingdom to earth and during the Last Supper, Jesus has more to say on what our role in achieving this will be.

Read Luke 22 v 24–27 and John 13 v 3–17, 31–35.

What are the key features of Jesus' Kingdom vision?

When a new owner takes over a business, changes to how things are done usually follow and Jesus' discussion with his disciples at the Last Supper bears a similar pattern, which is brought out in the passage from Luke. Jesus enters the argument the disciples are having about who is the greatest, by explaining how his kingdom operates on very different lines to the way the world does. In verse 25 Jesus says, 'In this world the kings and great men lord it over their people, yet they are called "friends of the people."' This last appellation is a translation for the Greek word *Euergétēs*, which means benefactor and it was a phrase rulers sometimes added to their own titles, such as the Egyptian king Ptolemy III Euergetes, who ruled between 246 and 222 BC. Yet such benefactors were not always so benevolent as they tried to appear and the commentaries for this verse have noted that 'those who were listening knew well how utterly false these high-sounding human titles often were.'[29] In the Greco-Roman world being a benefactor often involved the giving of gifts to obtain loyalty and honour, yet such generosity was frequently a thin concealment of the threat of harsh punishments for those who considered rebelling. In an era which embodied the notion of the might is right, Jesus' style of leadership differed considerably.

For God's kingdom vision to spread, it needed the right type of leaders, and Jesus touches on this in various places in the Gospels including Luke 22 v 26. Here he describes the sort of leader he is looking for: 'Those who are the greatest among you should take the lowest rank, and the leader should be like a servant.' A servant's heart though was a far cry from the culture Jesus was operating in. Charles Andrain and David Apter note Jesus' countercultural stance writing that:

> Asserting the priority of moral-spiritual values over material interests, Jesus contrasted Roman imperial domination with the Kingdom of God. Under the rule of Herod the Great [...] the government showed primary loyalty to Rome, not to the Jews. Herod built luxurious palaces, levied high taxes, exploited tenant farmers, and expropriated land that went to his absentee landlord friends. Cruelty, repression, and corruption prevailed. The Roman military ruled by coercive power, monopolised wealth in the few, and elevated their own status above the lowly.[30]

Conversely, leadership in God's kingdom, as Jesus tells his disciples at the Last Supper, is not about entitlement and privilege. Whilst John F. Kennedy famously said: 'ask not what your country can do for you, ask what you can do for your country', Jesus, centuries earlier, was exhorting his followers to an even greater challenge; namely to love others regardless of whether they were friends or foe. Once more this idea was antithetical to the culture of the period, with writers such as

Tacitus commenting that, 'Men are more ready to repay an injury than a benefit, because gratitude is a burden and revenge a pleasure.'[31]

Importantly though, Jesus roots his vision in his own actions. He certainly practised what he preached, which is exemplified in John 13 v 3–17. In this passage we have an account of Jesus washing his disciples' feet, an action of humility and service. Yet this action was not sycophantic or grovelling; adjectives which can often muddy our conceptions of what humility is about. Jesus' act of service is very much grounded in his identity and worth, as we read in verses 3–4 'Jesus knew that the Father had given him authority over everything and that he had come from God and would return to God. So he got up from the table, took off his robe, wrapped a towel around his waist, and poured water into a basin.'[32] The conjunction 'so' really is *so* important here! It is his awareness of who he is and the power he has that leads him to wash his followers' feet. Greatness does not preclude anyone from service, which Jesus signposted previously when he told his disciples in Matthew 20 v 28 that 'even the Son of Man came not to be served but to serve others and to give his life as a ransom for many.'

Again, Peter's perception that he knows best makes an appearance in this scene, as in verse 8 he refuses to let Jesus wash his feet. Peter unbeknownst to himself is refusing a lot more than a foot wash, as Jesus' washing of his disciples' feet is not just a model of a service but is a precursor to his immolation on the cross and the cleansing from sin that it would achieve for those who believed in it. So Peter's refusal at this point can be viewed as a rejection of God's grace, even if it is for the reason that he thinks he is not good enough to receive it. Yet this too is a form of pride and an important lesson from this scene with Peter is to know that God's kingdom vision can only be accomplished with God's grace working through us.

John's Gospel includes a long farewell speech from Jesus

(13 v 31–17 v 26), the beginning of which this chapter looks at. There are many examples of such speeches in the Old Testament, including ones given by Jacob, Moses, Joshua, Samuel and David, before they died. These speeches contained words of comfort, but also encouraged listeners to obey God and his laws and Jesus' own speech features these elements also. One of the first instructions he gives is this: 'So now I am giving you a new commandment: Love each other. Just as I have loved you, you should love each other.'[33]

How would you characterise Jesus' brand of love?

In the Jewish world love was not simply a temporary feeling, which fickly could be present or absent depending on your mood and situation. Instead, it is rooted in action. E. P. Sanders writes that 'in Jewish scripture and tradition the commandment to love is inseparable from the commandment to act. Love may include feeling, but in law it involves concrete and specific actions.'[34] Furthermore, Christopher Marshall reminds us that biblical love 'is a difficult undertaking that involves conscious effort, continual practice and considerable self-discipline' and that 'it is only because Jesus understood love in such activist terms that he could speak of loving one's enemies.'[35] It should be remembered that Jesus, following this command in verse 34, goes on to say that 'your love for one another will prove to the world that you are my disciples.' This is such an inspiring challenge, to love others in a radical way, that it draws attention and questions from those around us. It is a part of the fundamental core of Jesus' kingdom vision and how such a vision is to be unfolded throughout the world.

Jesus and You

The questions below are there to help you consider your own walk with God and the themes raised in this chapter. These questions touch upon sensitive subjects, so remember to listen to each other's responses with consideration and care.

Several of these questions are going to take us on a reflection of the Passover meal and our own lives.

Beginning with the Passover lamb, take time to think about what you have done this week or recently, that might have pulled you away from God. What failings do you need to put at the foot of the cross?

Next, considering the bread made without yeast, reflect on your 'old' life and your 'new' life in Jesus. How has your life changed? What aspects of the 'old' life do you still need to leave behind?

Moving on to the bitter greens, think about those times you have been hurt or betrayed by others. Are there still memories which cause a great deal of pain? If so, you may wish to bring these up in prayer privately or share them with someone you trust.

Finally, taking into account the kingdom vision presented during the Last Supper, how can you, individually or as a group or church, do more to see this kingdom extend its reach in your area or globally?

You might wish to consider this question in light of this quote from Beth Lindsay Templeton:

'Biblical love is commitment to another, no matter how good or bad, no matter how endearing or obnoxious. Biblical love is action, not feeling, a way of choosing rather than a way of reacting.'[36]

Endnotes

1. 1 Corinthians 10 v 16.
2. This is also known as the Passover meal.
3. Women and children were not excluded from participating in the festivals and in Deuteronomy 16 v 11 and 14, the Israelites during these festivals are encouraged to celebrate with their sons, daughters, orphans, widows, foreigners,

male and female servants and the Levites. Every adult, male or female, had the same spiritual obligations when it came to giving sacrifices to expiate their sins.

4. See Leviticus 17 v 11 and Hebrews 9 v 22.

5. Anon. (2008; 1996). 12:7 Footnote. In: *NLT Study Bible*. Illinois: Tyndale House Publishers. p. 143.

6. Cogen, M. (2017). Passover and the Atonement. In: Brock, D. and Glaser, M. *Messiah in the Passover*. Michigan: Chosen People Ministries. pp. 183–194 (p. 188).

7. See John 1 v 29.

8. Booker, R. (1987). *Jesus in the Feasts of Israel: Restoring the Spiritual Realities of the Feasts to the Church*. Pennsylvania: Destiny Image Publishers. p. 36.

9. Anon. (2013). Bitter Herbs. In: Longman III, Tremper *The Baker Illustrated Dictionary*. Michigan: Baker Books. p. 231.

10. 'I tell you the truth, unless you eat the flesh of the Son of Man and drink his blood, you cannot have eternal life within you. But anyone who eats my flesh and drinks my blood has eternal life, and I will raise that person at the last day.'

11. Pitre, B. (2011). *Jesus and the Jewish Roots of the Eucharist: Unlocking the Secrets of the Last Supper*. Doubleday: London. p. 75.

12. Migram, G. (2009). *Living Jewish Life Cycle: How to Create Meaningful Jewish Rites of Passage at Every Stage of Life*. Vermont: Jewish Lights Publishing. p. 8.

13. Eisenberg, R. (2008). *The JPS Guide to Jewish Traditions*. Philadelphia: The Jewish Publication Society.
However, other theories also exist including the four cups alluding to the four empires, Babylon, Media, Greece and Rome, whom Israel were ruled by post-Exodus.

14. For example, Exodus 6 v 6–7.

15. See Isaiah 53 v 7.

16. Booker, R. (1987). *Jesus in the Feasts of Israel: Restoring the*

Spiritual Realities of the Feasts to the Church. Pennsylvania: Destiny Image Publishers. p. 20.

17. See Exodus 12 v 22, Leviticus 1 v 15, Leviticus 5 v 9 and 1 Samuel 14 v 34.

18. Anon. (2008; 1996). 19:34 Footnote. In: *NLT Study Bible*. Illinois: Tyndale House Publishers. p. 1813.

19. 1 Peter 1 v 18–21.

20. See 1 John 1 v 7.

21. Booker, R. (1987). *Jesus in the Feasts of Israel: Restoring the Spiritual Realities of the Feasts to the Church*. Pennsylvania: Destiny Image Publishers. p. 27.

22. MacArthur, J. (2005). *The MacArthur Bible Commentary*. Nashville: Thomas Nelson. p. 35. This concept is also referred to in Jeremiah 34:18–19.

23. Hershey, D. (2011). *The Christian's Biblical Guide to Understanding Israel: Insight into God's Heart for His People*. Florida: Creation House. p. 36.

24. Anon. (2008; 1996). The New Covenant. In: *NLT Study Bible*. Illinois: Tyndale House Publishers. p. 1263.

25. See Luke 22 v 20.

26. See Hebrews 9 v 15 and 24.

27. See Hebrews 9 v 20.

28. Wright, T. (2001). *Luke for Everyone*. London: SPCK. p. 263.

29. Anon. (1883). *Luke 22:25 Pulpit Commentary*. Available: https://biblehub.com/commentaries/luke/22-25.htm. Last accessed 31st Aug 2020.

30. Andrain, C. and Apter D. (1995). *Political Protest and Social Change: Analysing Politics*. New York: New York University Press. p. 75.

31. Tacitus as quoted in Greene, R. (1998). *The 48 Laws of Power*. New York: Penguin Books. p. 12.

32. See also Philippians 2 v 6–8.

33. See John 13 v 34.

34. Sanders, E. P (1992). *Judaism: Practice and Belief 63BCE–66CE*.

London: SCM Press. p. 380.

35. Marshall, C. (2012). *Compassionate Justice: An Interdisciplinary Dialogue with Two Gospel Parables on Law, Crime, and Restorative Justice*. Oregon: Cascade Books. p. 72.

36. Templeton, B. (2008). *Loving Our Neighbour: A Thoughtful Approach to Helping in Poverty*. Indiana: iuniverse. p. 16.

Chapter 7

The Road Ahead

Post-Resurrection Dining

Philip asked, 'Do you understand what you are reading?'
The man replied, 'How can I, unless someone instructs me?'[1]

There are several parallels between the meals Jesus shared before and after his resurrection. They were still transformative occasions, during which Jesus turned accepted ideas and the status quo upside down. Before his crucifixion, Jesus had an enormous impact on people's lives, such as Zacchaeus and the woman who anointed his head. In his post-Resurrection dining we see Jesus doing the same for his disciples, especially Peter. As we will see, forgiveness remained a crucial aspect of the meals Jesus shared. However, it would be misleading to assume that nothing had changed; that Jesus was simply doing what he had always done. In this chapter we will be exploring the stories of the two disciples on the road to Emmaus, and Jesus' beach-set breakfast with his disciples, including Peter and John. Both meals show Jesus demonstrating how the new creation, which his death and resurrection inaugurated, was going to operate, and they also reveal Jesus empowering his disciples to continue his example of new creation living. In the story of the two disciples on the road to Emmaus we see Jesus' physical presence becoming more transitory, arguably preparing his disciples for his ascension. Yet in John's account of Jesus' reconciliation with Peter, we see that relational restoration is a deeply personal experience and Paula Gooder notes that John's Gospel is focused on depicting Jesus' 'resurrection from the perspective of [...] personal relationships'.[2] Whilst the way in which Jesus was interacting with his disciples changed after his resurrection, God had not stopped being a personal God, invested in humanity – warts and all. Peter's story resoundingly confirms this, reassuring us that even our sins can be used by God to further his Kingdom on earth.

Ice Breaker Questions

1. Describe a time when you felt very confused. For example, you could share about learning a topic for an exam, or an occasion when you were unsure of your future. What or who helped you get through this difficult period?
2. How easy do you find it to forgive others? What do you think is involved in forgiving another person?

Key Scriptures to Be Read

Luke 24 v 13–34

John 21 v 1–23

The Disciples on the Road to Emmaus

Re-read Luke 24 v 13–34.

What impediments to spiritual growth are there in the passage? How are these overcome?

Before looking at the meal the two disciples shared with Jesus, it is important to consider the situation they were in, and their state of mind, in order to see more clearly the role the meal will go on to play in their lives.

It has been three days since Jesus had been crucified and it has now been discovered that his body is missing. First by the women[3] and then confirmed by John and Peter.[4] The two disciples, unbeknownst to them, share all of this with Jesus himself. They then tell Jesus that the women also told them an angel had said Jesus was alive; but by the way they pass on this information, it does not sound like they believe it to be true. With the benefit of hindsight, it is easy for us to perceive Jesus' death not as an unfortunate end, but as the start of a glorious new beginning. This was not the case for the disciples at that moment. With their decision to leave Jerusalem, you could say these two disciples were literally retreating. Looking at various translations for verse 17, we can get a real sense of the distress they must have been experiencing, with the pair being described as: broken hearted, downcast, discouraged, and as a picture of gloom.[5] *The Message* particularly brings out the grief they were experiencing, writing that they were 'long-faced, like they had lost their best friend'. Yet Jesus was no ordinary best friend. They, along with many others, had placed a great deal of hope in Jesus being the Messiah they had been waiting so long for. But to them his death crushed this desperately desired expectation. There had been others who had promised freedom from the Romans and had claimed to have been anointed by God to rescue Israel from their oppressors.[6] But none of them had been able to fulfil their promises and they faced violent deaths. It had been hoped that Jesus was different, yet his similarly ignoble death seemed to put pains to that dream.

Perhaps this is why, days later, they were still intensely ruminating on what had happened in Jerusalem. Whilst the Bible advocates meditating on God's word[7] and keeping it fresh in our minds, the demeanour of the disciples, in this passage, suggests that this was not what they were doing on the road to Emmaus. Instead, it is likely that their discourse would have been repeatedly churning over the same details about Jesus' death. This post-mortem of events may have been started to try and make sense of what had happened, and as a way of dealing with their loss. There is nothing wrong with this. It is the sort of event you would want to understand more clearly! But the issue often associated with rumination is that it hinders problem-solving, as when we ruminate our thoughts are often negatively biased and they prevent us from seeing the information we are going over in a new light. Consequently, rumination can feel like you're going around in circles. It is not surprising with their human point of view and feelings that they were unable to develop further spiritually.

It is into this fog of confusion and emotions that Jesus enters. The importance of turning towards scripture in times of difficulty is reinforced in this instance, as after listening to their story, Jesus immediately reproves them, saying: 'You foolish people! You find it so hard to believe what the prophets wrote in the Scriptures. Wasn't it clearly predicted that the Messiah would have to suffer all these things before entering his glory?' As devout Jews, these scriptures would not have been unfamiliar to them, yet the penny had still not dropped that they had just been fulfilled. It is reading the scriptures in light of Jesus' resurrection, as well as his death, which enables believers to turn from despair to joy, as it is Jesus' resurrection which gives us our hope.

However, one barrier to growth the two disciples did not suffer from was an unwillingness to accept help and instruction.[8] Jesus had strong words for them, but that did not put them off listening to him and we are now going to explore further, how they went on to invite Jesus in to eat, an offer which also invited Jesus into their lives far more deeply than they could ever have imagined.

Bearing in mind what the disciples experienced on the road to Emmaus, what effect did their meal with Jesus have on them?

Hospitality is a core value established in the Old Testament, with precedents being found in Genesis 18, with Abraham and Sarah inviting three men to eat with them and take a rest from their journey. These were in fact messengers from God bringing Abraham news of the birth of his son. Later Hebrews 13 v 2 recalls this moment in its instruction to not 'forget to show hospitality to strangers, for some who have done this have entertained angels without realising it!' Paul Gooder notes that:

The word 'hospitality' has as one of its roots the Latin word 'hospes' which is related to the word for stranger and this is what ancient hospitality was all about. The act of welcoming a stranger into the home, caring for them, protecting them and sending them on their way strikes at the heart of many stories in the Bible...[9]

It is important to consider the theme of hospitality, in this story, as it is through the disciples' act of generosity that they then receive the most marvellous gift. When Jesus blesses and breaks the bread, their eyes are opened so they can not only recognise Jesus, know he is truly alive and has fulfilled God's promises, but that he is still present in their own lives. This is a powerful experience for the disciples, so it is rather fitting that the name of the place they were staying at, Emmaus, means warm springs, as looking back on their experience the disciples declare that their 'hearts burnt within' them when Jesus talked about the Scriptures.

The impact of this news is so momentous that despite the late hour they immediately travel straight back to Jerusalem to tell everyone. Their fear had been changed into courage, their despair into hope. Without their hospitality this transformation would not have happened. When considering what we can learn from this, Gooder writes that, as the disciples:

travelled with Jesus to Emmaus Jesus offered to them the untold riches of his own interpretation of scripture but the disciples were only able to realise the significance of this when they reached out to offer Jesus food and shelter. Only when they sought to give to him, could they truly receive what he offered. It is the paradox of true hospitality that in giving we receive and in welcoming strangers we find friendship, and that in the meeting the needs of a stranger, Jesus meets with us.[10]

So not only did this meal literally turn the disciples around to head back to Jerusalem, but Jesus also planted within them the tools to understand the scriptures. Not just to transform their own lives, but also the lives of others.

Read Genesis 3 v 6–7.

Compare this meal with the one the two disciples had with Jesus.

Comparing these two meals may feel like comparing chalk and cheese. In the first, Adam and Eve, disobey God and bring sin into the world, whilst the latter is one of the times Jesus appears post-crucifixion; proof that sin and therefore death had been defeated. The destruction wrought by the eating of the fruit of good and evil, contrasts to the restoration Jesus' death and resurrection brought. You can almost see them as bookends to the same story[11] and one phrase in particular unites them: 'their eyes were opened'.[12] When Adam and Eve ate the fruit, it opened their eyes, but it also opened them to 'shame at their nakedness'. They could make clothes for themselves, but they could not hide the damage they had done to their relationship with God. This is a moment of despair. Nothing could therefore be more different when the two disciples dine with Jesus. As he breaks bread with them 'suddenly, their eyes were opened and they recognised him' (Luke 24 v 31). Both this verse, and verse 16 of the same chapter use what is known as a divine passive. This is a structure within ancient Greek and is when God is 'the implied subject'[13] which means that it was God that prevented the two disciples from recognising Jesus on the road, but then opened their eyes during the meal. We should remember though that this was more than just a nice moment when someone recognises a friend they weren't expecting to be there. After all this is a friend who they thought was dead! It is a moment where the teachings Jesus shared with them on the road, as to his role within God's plan to rescue humanity, truly come alive. He is living proof that they are true, and that people can at last have their relationship with God restored. Jesus' resurrection is a sign that God's new creation had begun on earth, contrasting sharply with how the world had been polluted with sin in Genesis. The clean-up had commenced!

Jesus Reconciles with Peter

How do you think the disciples might have been feeling at the start of John 21? How does it change when they recognise Jesus? Are their reactions similar to those experienced by the two disciples discussed previously?

The disciples in this passage, like the two disciples we looked at in Luke 24, are also retreating, withdrawing back to their old lives and what they think they know. The direction of their lives has hit a wall, so going back to the familiar seems like a good solution. It is easy to picture them in their boat dejected and despondent, especially since they are not even able to catch any fish; something they thought they were at least good at. Similarly, like the two disciples on the road to Emmaus, the disciples in the boat do not immediately recognise Jesus. On this occasion Jesus uses a different action to bring about their recognition of him. He instructs them, knowing they have had an unsuccessful night of fishing, to try throwing out their nets again, in a new place. He did this the first time he met Peter, John and James[14] and it led to them leaving their old lives behind to follow him. So when he recalls the disciples to this past event, he is inviting them once more to commit to him. Recognition, as with the disciples on the road to Emmaus, produces a powerful reaction. The intensity of this moment can be seen in Peter's response when he throws himself into the water to reach Jesus, unable to wait for the boat to be brought in to shore. We have seen Peter's enthusiasm turn sour in the past, but in this instance, it is the beginning of poignant reconciliation.

How did Peter become estranged from Jesus?

In the previous chapter we considered the motivations behind Peter's betrayal of Jesus. He was confident in his own ability to stand by Jesus, no matter what. You could say he was proud of it. Others may fall away, but not him. Yet as we know, Jesus is not fooled for a moment, and warns Peter that he will deny him three times before the cock has crowed. As this comes to pass the painfulness of this scene is intensified when we bear in mind that Peter was not making his denials far removed from Jesus. Peter has been able to follow Jesus into the High Priest's courtyard and the most painful part of this event is recorded in Luke 22 v 61, when Peter has spoken his final denial of Jesus: 'At that moment the Lord turned and looked at Peter.' There is nothing secret or private about Peter's betrayal.

How does Jesus go about forgiving Peter? Describe the process mentioned in John 21 v 1–23. How does Jesus' approach differ from our own?

One of the most striking aspects of Jesus' approach to forgiving Peter is in his choice of words. We might expect Jesus to express how sad, disappointed or angry he was with Peter. We might anticipate Peter being made to feel bad about what he has done and having to promise not to do it again. Yet Jesus does not treat Peter like a naughty child, who will have to pay for a broken window out of his own pocket money. Jesus does not indulge in purposeless recrimination, in order to assuage his own hurt feelings, like we might do. Alternatively, Jesus' approach to forgiving Peter has a long-term perspective; one which sees Peter transformed from remaining paralysed in guilt and instead enabled to promote God's kingdom, now relying on God's strength rather than his own.

Instead of asking Peter if he is sorry, three times Jesus asks Peter if he loves him and after each of Peter's replies Jesus commissions him to 'take care of my sheep'. Paula Gooder writes that this 'command turns Peter outwards. His expression of love is not to show piety or worship to Jesus but to care for Jesus' flock'.[15] She goes on to emphasise how:

> In our modern world, the word love has become almost entirely associated with emotion. 'Do you love me?' is a question that asks for a response based on feelings. In the ancient world, emotion was important, but not as important as action.[16]

Emotions can be quite inward looking, whilst action forces our attention outwards and onto the needs of others. Yet such a shift in focus does not leave us unaffected. In the way the two disciples on the road to Emmaus received deep understanding from Jesus, once they had invited him to dinner, we can also see a similar process playing out here. It is in giving out that Peter will receive and this whole encounter shows how forgiveness can be an enabling experience for the person who has done wrong. It provides them with the invitation to change. Robert J. Schreiter explores this further when he comments that:

> The vocation to which the reconciled person is called often has a dual connection. There is a connection back to the experience of violence. Such is the case, for example, when reconciled survivors of violence work with other victims of violence. It is part of remembering in a different way. The other connection looks forward, often to work so that the conditions that permitted the violence to occur do not happen again. We see this dual connection in the commissioning of Peter. He, who once denied knowing Jesus is now charged with keeping Jesus' memory alive in the community of disciples. He whose denial betrayed trust is now entrusted with the little flock of Jesus' lambs. His vocation, his commission, allows Peter to remember his own past in a different way, and to help create

a community where trust is nurtured so that denial will never happen again.[17]

This process is played out in C. S. Lewis' Narnia series through the character of Edmund Pevensie. Like Peter, in *The Lion, The Witch and The Wardrobe* (1950) Edmund betrays his siblings and he also becomes a traitor towards Aslan's kingdom. Yet that is not the end of his story. Aslan goes to great lengths to redeem Edmund and spare him from the punishment which rightly awaits him according to the laws of the land. Ultimately, he goes on to fight in Aslan's army and fight against the White Witch; who at the very start he had viewed so favourably as a person through whom he could gain supreme power. But by the end of the book, authority is bestowed upon him by Aslan instead, giving a very different kind of power. He is crowned alongside his brothers and sisters and he is named King Edmund the Just; a title which does not look back to his past, but to the future and in later books his experience of being lost and then restored, has a profound impact on his actions. It is perhaps because of his great fall that he is one of the characters who grows the most over the series. In *Prince Caspian* (1951) when they are deciding which direction to go in next, Edmund is the only one who backs Lucy's choice, (which she bases on having seen Aslan). When it comes to disbelief, he describes himself as having been 'the worst of the lot'[18] last time. Whilst in *The Horse and His Boy* (1954), his own experience of being forgiven for a grave crime influences his advice to King Lune to not behead Rabadash. He backs up his stance by saying, 'But even a traitor may mend. I have known one that did.'[19] His compassion similarly extends to his cousin Eustace in *The Voyage of the Dawn Treader* (1952), who upon recovering from his own unwise decisions is told by Edmund that he was not 'as bad as I was on my first trip to Narnia. You were only an ass, but I was a traitor'.[20]

Nevertheless, offering second chances, does not come

without risk. Reading the passage from John, you might think it foolhardy of Jesus to offer Peter such a big and important assignment. Sheep and lambs are vulnerable creatures, prey to many dangers – and Jesus' followers are not much different. Peter has shown himself to be unreliable under pressure and to speak before he thinks. How could Jesus trust Peter to do the job he has been given? Thankfully for Peter, and for us, Jesus' trust is not based on our past conduct nor our current merits and the Bible includes a catalogue of questionable people who were chosen by God to do a specific task.

God does not need us to do anything, yet from as early as Genesis God decided to involve humans in the restoration process. Returning to John 21, we can see this symbolised in Jesus' actions. In verse 9 we are told that the disciples 'found breakfast waiting for them' when they came ashore. From a practical point of view Jesus did not need any of the fish the disciples caught. Yet in the next verse he still asks them to bring some of their fish, and today God still asks us to bring him whatever resource or gift we have, however small it seems, for him to use in ways we can often not anticipate. Similarly, Jesus did not have to commission Peter, but again he still did so. This reveals an important facet to God as when He involves us in his work, this very process enables us to change; not to become less ourselves, but more and in doing so come to reflect more truly God's image, whose likeness we are made in.

However, this transformation is an ongoing one, the people God chooses to help spread his kingdom are imperfect vessels and it does not take long for this same passage from John to prove this point. Jesus has directed Peter's attention outwards, to support and help develop the future church. Yet in verses 20–23 Peter's outward focus very quickly needs adjusting, as his attention strays to wanting to know the fate of another disciple, John. This is not what looking outwards is supposed to be about, though the temptation to do so is very easy to succumb to. Comparing himself to others, and assessing what God has in store for them, is not what Jesus wants Peter to focus on, as just like rumination for the two disciples on the road to Emmaus, it is another mindset which hinders spiritual growth and our relationship with God.

Jesus and You

The questions below are there to help you consider your own walk with God and the themes raised in this chapter. These questions touch upon sensitive subjects, so remember to listen to each other's responses with consideration and care.

1. This chapter has looked at two occasions when people recognise God's presence. In what ways have you noticed God's presence at work in your life?

2. In addition, you may wish to consider what you might say to those who are unsure of how to see God at work in their lives.

3. In John 21 v 15 Jesus asks Peter, 'Do you love me more than these?' Think about the things and people that fill your life. Are there any taking priority or precedence over God in your life at the moment?

4. Spend some time with God reflecting on your answer.

5. The two passages we have explored in this chapter also show some examples of things which can impede our spiritual growth, such as negative emotions, unhelpful rumination and comparing ourselves to others. Reflect upon your own life. Consider what might be hindering your walk with God.

6. If you are discussing this in your small group, you may wish to split into pairs to share your answers and then pray about them with each other. Alternatively, if your small group does not feel comfortable with this, you could make sharing more anonymous by having each

member write their answer down. These answers could be mixed up before being shared. Whilst it is important to encourage everyone to participate, group leaders should not pressurise for a response.

7.   For some Christians it can be hard for them to believe that God can and does want to work through them. Often, they can feel their past sins exclude them from doing so. How can such people take comfort and hope from Peter's story?

Endnotes

1.   Acts 8 v 30–31.

2.   Gooder, Paula (2009). *This Risen Existence: The Spirit of Easter*. Norwich: Canterbury Press. p. 28.

3.   The Gospel accounts vary on exactly how many women went along, although Mary Magdalene is cited in three of the four Gospels.

4.   See John 20 v 1–10.

5.   In order of appearances these words and phrases come from the *Amplified Bible, Complete Jewish Bible, Christian Standard Bible* and the *New Testament for Everyone*.

6.   Not every Messiah claimant was suggesting they were God in human form, but they did all suggest that they had God's anointing to save Israel. Examples include Athronges, Simon of Peraea and Judas the Galilean, who had all led rebellions in and around the time of Jesus' birth and early years.

7.   For example, see Joshua 1 v 8, Psalm 119 v 115 and Philippians 4 v 8.

8.   A willingness to accept instruction and to have the Scriptures explained can also be found in Philip's encounter with the Ethiopian eunuch in Acts 8 v 26–40.

9.   Gooder, Paula (2009). *This Risen Existence: The Spirit of Easter*. Norwich: Canterbury Press. p. 47.

10. *Ibid*, p. 48.

11. We see something similar happen with Peter's betrayal of Jesus and his reconciliation to him. Peter is standing beside a charcoal fire when he denies knowing Jesus three times. But it is by another charcoal fire that Peter's relationship to Jesus is restored. The charcoal fire may bring back painful memories for Peter, but as Jesus walks him through them, asking him three times if Peter loves him, Jesus redeems Peter and lets the sins of his past become an important moment of spiritual growth. The presence of burning coals in both Peter's downfall and redemption remind us of the dual symbolism of combustion: that of destruction and purification. If Peter was to become the rock Jesus would build his church on, then his impetuous behaviour would need to change. The presence of the burning coal also echoes Isaiah 6 v 5–7 in which Isaiah declares himself 'doomed, for I am a sinful man. I have filthy lips' – a sin which reminds us of Peter's predicament. Yet just like Peter, Isaiah is not left in this unredeemed place, and he writes that a 'seraphim flew to me with a burning coal he had taken from the altar with a pair of tongs. He touched my lips with it and said, "See, this coal has touched your lips. Now your guilt is removed, and your sins are forgiven."'

12. See Genesis 3 v 7 and Luke 24 v 31.

13. Anon. (2008; 1996). 24:16 Footnote. In: *NLT Study Bible*. Illinois: Tyndale House Publishers. p. 1761.

14. See Luke 5.

15. Gooder, Paula (2009). *This Risen Existence: The Spirit of Easter*. Norwich: Canterbury Press. p. 62.

16. *Ibid*, p. 62.

17. Schreiter, R. (1998). *The Ministry of Reconciliation: Spirituality and Strategies*. New York: Orbis Books. pp. 91–92.

18. Lewis, C. S. (1951; 1997). *Prince Caspian*. London: Collins. p. 112.

19. Lewis, C. S. (1954; 1997). *The Horse and His Boy*. London: Collins. p. 167.
20. Lewis, C. S. (1952). *The Voyage of the Dawn Treader*. London: Collins. p. 87.

Author Biography

Kate Jackson has always lived in the North of England, and from an early age developed three strong passions: animals, teaching, and golden age crime fiction. She lives in a beautiful rural area with Agatha her rescue cat, 14 rare breed chickens and a small herd of pygmy goats. Kate's love of helping others grow led her to completing a PGCE with a Literacy and ESOL specialism after her English degree, during which time she supported refugees and asylum seekers in learning English. She has also published two puzzle books: *The Pocket Detective* (2018) and *The Pocket Detective 2* (2019). For the past four years she has been teaching in her Christian house group and has created Lent materials for her local Methodist church and these experiences have influenced the writing of this study guide.

Note to Reader

Thank you for buying a copy of *Dining with Jesus*. I hope this study guide has aided you in digging deeper into the Bible and that the skills you have gained or honed through reading it will be useful in your future studying of God's word. If you have the time, it would be greatly appreciated if you could add a review of my study guide online, be it on a personal blog, the website you purchased it from, social media, or on any website you use to record and share your personal reading.

Sincerely,

K. J.

Bibliography

Andrain, C. and Apter D. (1995). *Political Protest and Social Change: Analysing Politics.* New York: New York University Press.

Anon. (2012; 1970). *A Survey of the New Testament.* 5th ed. Michigan: Zondervan.

Anon. (2013). Banquet. In: Longman III, Tremper *The Baker Illustrated Dictionary.* Michigan: Baker Books.

Anon. (1990). Decapolis. In: Mills, Watson E. *Mercer Dictionary of the Bible.* Georgia: Mercer University Press.

Anon. (2008; 1996). *NLT Study Bible.* Illinois: Tyndale House Publishers.

Anon. (1883). *Luke 22:25 Pulpit Commentary.* Available: https://biblehub.com/commentaries/luke/22-25.htm. Last accessed 31st Aug 2020.

Anon. (2011). Sign #4 – Jesus Feeds the Five Thousand (6:1-15). In: Hays, J. and Duvall, J. *The Baker Illustrated Bible Handbook.* Michigan: Baker Books.

Anon. (2010). IX The Rise of Judaism. In: Tenney, M. C. *The Zondervan Encyclopedia of the Bible Volume 3 H–L Revised.* Michigan: Zondervan.

Aus, Roger David (2010). *Feeding the Five Thousand: Studies in the Judaic Background of Mark 6:30–44 par. and John 6:1–15.* Maryland: University Press of America.

Black, M. (1967). *An Aramaic Approach to the Gospels and Acts.* Oxford: Clarendon.

Booker, R (1987). *Jesus in the Feasts of Israel: Restoring the Spiritual Realities of the Feasts to the Church.* Pennsylvania: Destiny Image Publishers.

Brown, Rev J. (1833). *A Dictionary of the Holy Bible.* New York: J & J Harper.

Caird, G. B. (1994). *New Testament Theology.* Oxford: Clarendon

Press.

Cogen, M. (2017). Passover and the Atonement. In: Brock, D. and Glaser, M. *Messiah in the Passover*. Michigan: Chosen People Ministries.

Conner, C. J. (2007). *Jesus and the Culture Wars: Reclaiming the Lord's Prayer*. Oklahoma: Tate Publishing.

Cross, David (2008). *Trapped by Control: How to Find Freedom*. Lancaster: Ellel Ministries.

Eisenberg, R. (2008). *The JPS Guide to Jewish Traditions*. Philadelphia: The Jewish Publication Society.

Evans, Craig A. (2011; 1990). *Understanding the Bible Commentary Series: Luke*. Michigan: Zondervan.

Fairchild, Mary. (2019). *Table of Showbread*. Available: https://www.learnreligions.com/table-of-showbread-700114. Last accessed 15th April 2020.

France, R. T. (2007). *The New International Commentary on the New Testament: The Gospel of Matthew*. Michigan: William B Eerdmans Publishing Company.

Fryman, June (2018). *Meaning of 'I am the bread of life'*. Available: https://www.wnewsj.com/opinion/columns/83226/meaning-of-i-am-the-bread-of-life. Last accessed 16th April 2020.

Gooder, Paula (2009). *This Risen Existence: The Spirit of Easter*. Norwich: Canterbury Press.

Gundry, Robert H. (2012; 1970). *A Survey of the New Testament*. 5th ed. Michigan: Zondervan.

Hershey, D. (2011). *The Christian's Biblical Guide to Understanding Israel: Insight into God's Heart for His People*. Florida: Creation House.

Hoehner, H. (1977; 2010). *Chronological Aspects of the Life of Christ*. Michigan: Zondervan Academic.

Hurtado, Larry (1989; 2011). *Understanding the Bible Commentary Series: Mark*. Michigan: Baker Books.

Isaak, J. (2011). *New Testament Theology: Extending the Table*.

Oregon: Cascade Books.

Jeffers, James S. (2000). *The Greco-Roman World of the New Testament Era: Exploring the Background of Early Christianity*. Illinois: Intervarsity-Press.

Kendall, R. T. (2004). *The Parables of Jesus: A Guide to Understanding and Applying the Stories Jesus Told*. Michigan: Chosen Books.

Kohn, R. & Rebecca Moore (2007). *A Portable God: The Origin of Judaism and Christianity*. Plymouth: Rowman and Littlefield Publishers, Inc.

Köstenberger, A. (2004). *John*. Michigan: Barker Academic.

Ktav, S. (1987). *A Rabbinic Commentary on the New Testament: The Gospels of Matthew, Mark and Luke*. New Jersey: Publishing House Inc.

Lane, W. (1974). *The Gospel of Mark*. Michigan: Wm. B. Eerdmans Publishing Co.

Levi, R. *Pesachim 68b:13*. Available: https://www.sefaria. org/Jerusalem_Talmud_Pesachim.68b.13. Last accessed 06/08/2021.

Lewis, C. S. (1951; 1997). *Prince Caspian*. London: Collins.

Lewis, C. S. (1952; 1997). *The Voyage of the Dawn Treader*. London: Collins.

Lewis, C. S. (1954; 1997). *The Horse and His Boy*. London: Collins.

Lewis, C. S. (1956; 1997). *The Last Battle*. London: Collins.

MacArthur, J. (2005). *The MacArthur Bible Commentary*. Nashville: Thomas Nelson.

Marshall, C. (2012). *Compassionate Justice: An Interdisciplinary Dialogue with Two Gospel Parables on Law, Crime, and Restorative Justice*. Oregon: Cascade Books.

Migram, G. (2009). *Living Jewish Life Cycle: How to Create Meaningful Jewish Rites of Passage at Every Stage of Life*. Vermont: Jewish Lights Publishing.

Nave, G. (2002). *The Role and Function of Repentance in Luke-Acts*. Boston: Society of Biblical Literature.

Nickel, D. (2014). *A Day in the Life of Jesus*. Georgia: TEACH

Services.

Phillips, J. B. (1952; 2004). *Your God is Too Small*. New York: Touchstone.

Phillips, R. (2015). *The Kingdom According to Jesus: A Study of Jesus' Parables on the Kingdom of Heaven*. Indiana: WestBow Press.

Pitre, B. (2011). *Jesus and the Jewish Roots of the Eucharist: Unlocking the Secrets of the Last Supper*. Doubleday: London.

Posterski, D. (2013). *Jesus on Justice: Living Lives of Compassion and Conviction*. Ontario: World Vision Canada.

Poythress, Vern S. (2016). *The Miracles of Jesus: How the Saviour's Mighty Acts Serve as Signs of Redemption*. Illinois: Crossway.

Sanders, E. P. (1992). *Judaism: Practice and Belief 63BCE–66CE*. London: SCM Press.

Schreiter, R. (1998). *The Ministry of Reconciliation: Spirituality and Strategies*. New York: Orbis Books.

Spurgeon, C. (2008). November 12. In: Reimann, J. *Look Unto Me: The Devotions of Charles Spurgeon*. Michigan: Zondervan.

Strohman, J. (2012; 2015). *Application Commentary of the Gospel of Matthew*. San Diego: Cross Centred Press.

Suetonius. (1996). Life of Vespasian 1–2. In: ed. Lomas, K. *Roman Italy, 338 BC–AD 200: A Sourcebook*. London: Routledge.

Tacitus. In: Greene, R. (1998). *The 48 Laws of Power*. New York: Penguin Books.

Templeton, B. (2008). *Loving Our Neighbour: A Thoughtful Approach to Helping in Poverty*. Indiana: iuniverse.

Thomas, R. L. & Gundry, S. N. (1978). *A Harmony of the Gospels*. Illinois: Moody Press.

Volf, M. (1996). *Exclusion & Embrace: A Theological Exploration of Identity, Otherness, and Reconciliation*. Nashville: Abingdon Press.

William, Matthew C. (2011). Gospel of John. In: Hays, J. and Duvall, J. *The Baker Illustrated Bible Handbook*. Michigan: Baker Books.

Wink, Walter (1992; 2017). *Engaging the Powers: 25th Anniversary Edition*. Minneapolis: Fortress Press.

Wright, N. T. and Michael F. Bird (2019). *The New Testament in Its World: An Introduction to the History, Literature, and Theology of the First Christians*. London: Harper Collins. p. 209.

Wright, T. (2001). *John for Everyone: Part 1 Chapters 1–10*. London: SPCK.

Wright, T. (2001). *Luke for Everyone*. London: SPCK.

Wright, T. (2001). *Mark for Everyone*. London: SPCK.

Wright, T. (2002). *Matthew for Everyone: Part 1*. London: SPCK.

Wright, T. (2002). *Matthew for Everyone: Part 2*. London: SPCK.

Yancy, P. (2009). January 14th Undesirables. In: *Grace Notes: Daily Readings with a Fellow Pilgrim*. Michigan: Zondervan.

CIRCLE
BOOKS

CHRISTIAN FAITH

Circle Books explores a wide range of disciplines within the field of Christian faith and practice. It also draws on personal testimony and new ways of finding and expressing God's presence in the world today.
If you have enjoyed this book, why not tell other readers by posting a review on your preferred book site. Recent bestsellers from Circle Books are:

I Am With You (Paperback)
John Woolley
These words of divine encouragement were given to John Woolley in his work as a hospital chaplain, and have since inspired and uplifted tens of thousands, even changed their lives.
Paperback: 978-1-90381-699-8 ebook: 978-1-78099-485-7

God Calling
A. J. Russell
365 messages of encouragement channelled from Christ to two anonymous "Listeners".
Hardcover: 978-1-905047-42-0 ebook: 978-1-78099-486-4

The Long Road to Heaven,
A Lent Course Based on the Film
Tim Heaton
This second Lent resource from the author of *The Naturalist and the Christ* explores Christian understandings of "salvation" in a five-part study based on the film *The Way*.
Paperback: 978-1-78279-274-1 ebook: 978-1-78279-273-4

Abide In My Love
More Divine Help for Today's Needs
John Woolley
The companion to *I Am With You*, *Abide In My Love* offers words of divine encouragement.
Paperback: 978-1-84694-276-1

From the Bottom of the Pond
The Forgotten Art of Experiencing God in the Depths of the Present Moment
Simon Small
From the Bottom of the Pond takes us into the depths of the present moment, to the only place where God can be found.
Paperback: 978-1-84694-066-8 ebook: 978-1-78099-207-5

God Is A Symbol Of Something True
Why You Don't Have to Choose Either a Literal Creator God or a Blind, Indifferent Universe
Jack Call
In this examination of modern spiritual dilemmas, Call offers the explanation that some of the most important elements of life are beyond our control: everything is fundamentally alright.
Paperback: 978-1-84694-244-0

The Scarlet Cord

Conversations With God's Chosen Women
Lindsay Hardin Freeman, Karen N. Canton
Voiceless wax figures no longer, twelve biblical women,
outspoken, independent, faithful, selfless risk-takers, come to life
in *The Scarlet Cord*.
Paperback: 978-1-84694-375-1

Will You Join in Our Crusade?

The Invitation of the Gospels Unlocked by the Inspiration of
Les Miserables
Steve Mann
Les Miserables' narrative is entwined with Bible study in this book
of 42 daily readings from the Gospels, perfect for Lent or anytime.
Paperback: 978-1-78279-384-7 ebook: 978-1-78279-383-0

A Quiet Mind

Uniting Body, Mind and Emotions in Christian Spirituality
Eva McIntyre
A practical guide to finding peace in the present moment that will
change your life, heal your wounds and bring you a quiet mind.
Paperback: 978-1-84694-507-6 ebook: 978-1-78099-005-7

Readers of ebooks can buy or view any of these bestsellers by
clicking on the live link in the title. Most titles are published in
paperback and as an ebook. Paperbacks are available in traditional
bookshops. Both print and ebook formats are available online.

Find more titles and sign up to our readers' newsletter at http://
www.johnhuntpublishing.com/christianity. Follow us on Facebook
at https://www.facebook.com/ChristianAlternative.